BREAK THE *food* RULES:

Unleashing Your Natural Ability to Eat Intuitively, Listen Your Gut & Feel Great

By Dr. Lauryn Lax

Edited by Jyssica Schwartz
www.jyssicaschwartz.com

Dedication

This is for you, mom, dad, Ashley and Jared. My cheer squad who *never* gave up on me.

And this is also for you reading this, dear sister. You is strong. You is smart. You is capable of great things when you listen to your gut... Your intuition.

Table of Contents

Introduction

Mickey Mouse Pancakes
Do a Body Good

When I was little, my mom would cook chocolate chip pancakes every year for my birthday.

And not just any chocolate chip pancakes, but *Mickey Mouse* chocolate chip pancakes.

I eagerly anticipated my happy Mickey Mouse pancakes, drizzled with a touch of Aunt Jemima syrup and smiling back at me from my special "Birthday Girl" plate with a candle for each eye.

Mom would serve me breakfast in bed like a queen, as she, my dad, little brother, and sister all serenaded me with the "Happy Birthday" song. I'd make a thoughtful wish, blow out the candles with as much gusto as I could muster, and then enjoy every sticky, sweet, syrupy, chocolatey, fluffy bite of my once-a-year Mickey Mouse pancake— no cares, worries or thoughts in the world, except... *feeling good, like really good.* **Better than good. Feeling *like a million bucks.***

Beyond the sugary party in my mouth, my "feel good" feelings went far deeper than the food I ate.

Feeling good was really all about feeling *loved, nourished, cared for, and totally connected to my own worth (my amazing, one-year-wiser birthday girl self).*

Every year, my birthday pancakes reminded me of just how loved and uniquely, wonderfully special I was simply for being born—no strings attached. And Mom's thoughtful hands and heart behind my mouse-shaped flapjacks was like insurance for my self worth. I *knew* I was *simply enough* by being me (and having a birthday) and I totally rocked that!

Unfortunately, those happy Mickey Mouse pancake moments abruptly ended after my 9th birthday, when I embarked on a 15-year-long struggle (ages 9 to 24) with eating disorders and the diet mentality—an all-out brawl with food, my body, and fitness.

It all went down one day at recess. When four other little girls and myself gathered in a circle together and the topic of weight came up.

"Oh my gosh you guys, I weighed myself last night and I am 69 pounds! I am so fat," the Queen-Bee of the crew said. We all, of course, were desperate to be accepted by the Queen Bee and although she saw herself as fat, we saw her as perfect. "No! No! No!" the other little girls and I chimed in. "You're not fat at all!" To which she responded, "Well if I am not fat, then how much do you guys weigh?!" And, one by one, each of us went around the circle, reporting to the Queen Bee our exact weight. Ashamed of my (healthy) 80 pounds for a 10 year-old girl my height, I looked down at my feet when the question came to me and replied, "I have no idea. I haven't weighed myself in a long time."

Game. Set. Match.

I went home, stood in my pantry in the kitchen, and vowed to myself I would go on a diet to lose 10 pounds and become the *best version of myself* I could be.

Before I knew it though, something else took hold of my mind, and what began as an innocent diet, turned into an all-out war with my body, fitness and food—Mickey Mouse pancakes included.

During that long, dark season, I stopped believing that I was as special as my mom and dad, birthday songs and Mickey Mouse pancakes made me feel on those birthdays. And I spent 15+ years at war with **every piece of me**—hating my nose, my thighs, wishing I looked like someone else, wanting someone else's life or job or abs, overanalyzing every morsel of food I ate or exercise routine I followed, and straight-up longing to just *feel good* (and be *good enough*) in my own skin.

Fast forward to today.

This year, on my 30th birthday to be exact—now over 20 years removed from when my battle with food, my body and fitness began—I ate a Mickey Mouse pancake.

While I no longer live at home and cook for myself nowadays, I *wanted* a Mickey Mouse pancake. So that's what I did.

I whipped up my own updated rendition of my favorite banana-chocolate chip (Mickey Mouse-shaped) pancakes, then topped it with an extra smear of sunbutter and crispy turkey bacon.

And you know what?

I enjoyed every bite.

Today Mickey Mouse pancakes mean freedom—freedom from food rules, insecurities about being "good enough," and calorie counting in the back of my mind.

Eating that Mickey Mouse pancake on my 30th birthday signified one thing: I feel GOOD in my own skin (really good). And those feel-good feelings run far deeper than any chocolate chip, growl in my stomach, sweaty workout session or number on a scale can give me.

I feel good—deep down—regardless of what my body looks like, how many calories I eat, or whether or not I've followed the rules. In fact, I feel a little bit better when I break some rules.

Over the past 20 years that food "issues" and body "issues" have been part of my life (both in my sickness, and now in my health helping others with these things), I've been on a journey to discover what it means to **feel good—at home, at peace, and totally connected**—in your own body.

What it means to *feel good enough* simply for being *me*—no 250,000 Instagram followers, perfectly curvaceous Kim Kardashian body, commercial-worthy skin, teeth and hair, or six-pack abs necessary.

What I've discovered? **Feeling good goes beyond weight, food and fitness. And feeling good goes far beyond anyone else's approval.**

Pop quiz: What does *"feeling good"* mean to you?

Is it:

- Fitting into your jeans?
- Not feeling bloated?
- Walking confidently in your favorite pumps and pencil skirt, head up, like you own the place?
- Speaking your mind and not caring so much about what others think?
- Having energy without needing coffee in the mornings?
- Getting into a groove or routine that keeps you motivated and pumped?
- Feeling loved and connected to your community?
- Being in a relationship which is a two-way street - love and thoughtfulness for one another - with a partner who totally encourages you?
- An endorphin rush after a sweaty run on the trail?
- Being totally in your "element" or "flow" and doing things you love in your life, nothing holding you down?
- Working at a job where you feel valued and appreciated?

While every individual has a completely different and unique definition of what "feeling good" means to them, chances are that "feeling good" in your own skin is about so much more than eating the "right amount" of calories, steps on your FitBit, sticking to diet rules, checking off your bikini body workout routine, ordering an entree based upon your food fears, or trying a 21-day detox.

*Disclaimer: It's **NOT** bad to want to look good, or feel good, but as you'll soon discover, the key to unlocking both of these desires has **nothing** to do with diet rules, workout programs, juice cleanses or any other rules we've made ourselves follow.*

Instead, "feeling good" has *everything* to do with CONNECTING to *yourself* - from the inside out (mind, body and soul) - and becoming more intuitive! (A language you've known all along).

You were born knowing how to *feel good.*

As a child, you LOVED feeling good and balanced, and when you didn't feel good or balanced, you **knew** what to do:

- You ate when you were hungry.
- You stopped when you were full.
- You played when you had energy.
- You napped when you were exhausted.
- You spoke up for yourself (or your friend) on the playground when a bully tried to take your lunch money or uninvite you to their birthday party.
- You cried when you needed a diaper change.
- And you ate Mickey Mouse pancakes, because gosh darn it, you liked Mickey Mouse pancakes and felt special for just being YOU on your big day.

You knew how to connect, listen, and honor your body and how to go with your gut.

Then, life happened.

Being a grown-up happened. A lot of noise (in the diet, food and fitness worlds) happened. And, many times, you forgot *how* to listen to your body or go with your gut.

Until now...

In this book, I will share with you my simple **5-Step Thrive Method** for unleashing your body's natural ability to eat and move intuitively, listen to your gut, and feel good in your own skin. (No food rules, fad workouts or green juice required).

Are you are tired of Googling topics like: "How to lose or gain weight," "Cure bloating and constipation," or "Number of calories or carbs in _____ (insert food)"? Exhausted from consulting doctors, trainers, 30-day programs or self-help books that can't seem to help you figure out how to "hack" or change your health? Want to be done obsessing over thoughts about food, fitness or your body?

Then you've come to the right place.

It's time to write a new story in what it takes to *feel good,* and become the *best version of yourself.*

It's time to break some rules.

Starting with understanding what rules you've been believing in the first place...

"When I Lose 10 Pounds"

"When I lose 10 pounds, then _____."

Then what? You fill in the blank.

You'll be happy?
You'll love my body?
You'll feel more confident?
You'll fit into my bridesmaid's dress better?
You'll be the one that got away?
You'll get more respect from people?
You'll respect yourself more?

The idea of "when I lose 10 pounds" has been a battle cry of human-kind from the beginning of time, the crazy idea that "the grass is greener on the other side" (and *life will be better if only I were to be thinner, fitter, prettier, etc."*).

Whether you want to lose 10 pounds, gain 10 pounds, lean out, tone up, get a better job, make more money, have cuter clothes, get married, have babies, break free from your babies for the night, or any other "dangling carrot," we have all fallen into the belief that our life will be *so much better if we just had that <u>one thing</u> we want.*

In our current culture, those "10 pounds" are the one thing standing between us and success.

Weight Watchers commercials play on repeat to remind us we can "live fully" if we shape up and slim down. Magazine covers in the checkout line display the same stories every month, with different bikini-clad models showing their six packs, and articles on how to "Look Great Naked," "Get Flat Abs Now!" and "Drop 2 Dress Sizes this Week!"

Food products and menus boast "gluten-free," "high protein," and "low calorie," reminding us that we should make "wise choices" if we want that body.

Every time we go to slip on our favorite pair of skinny jeans or yoga pants, we are reminded by the little voice in the back of our heads that we are not 100% where we want to be, that they would look better if we just had less of a tummy or smaller thighs.

Glancing at pictures from your past, like high school prom, college Rush, and your wedding always makes you think, "If only I looked like that again!"

As you look through your Instagram feed, comparing yourself to other beauties in the world of social media, which triggers an inner dissatisfaction with yourself: *I want to be that girl.*

Newsflash: You don't really want to lose those 10 pounds.

You want that **<u>FEELING</u>** of losing those 10 pounds.

That feeling of: Confidence. Radiance. Seemingly no care in the world. Peace with yourself and in your own skin. Health and balance—in all areas of your life—not just your body.

What do those 10 pounds (or stylish wardrobe, or man on your arm, or money in your bank, or job freedom) *really give you?*

Try to get into the "headspace" of yours and figure out what those 10 pounds mean to you.

"If I were 10 pounds (lighter or heavier), I would *feel* _____."

Or, "If I lost x-amount of body fat, then I would *feel* _____."

Pinpoint what it is you are really wanting.

If there's one thing I've learned in my own life—it is that there will **ALWAYS** be "dangling carrots" when we remain focused and motivated by external validation and successes alone.

Whenever those 10 pounds are lost, we will still have something else we want more (a tighter body, a more chiseled waist, five more pounds, better Instagram photos, etc.), and never fully satisfied.

In our efforts to be more satisfied, we turn to more rules, waste time on Google, spend hundreds of dollars on trainers, supplements and books, and continue internally beating ourselves up—only to to fall short.

Do you ever wonder *why* you still want to lose 10 pounds or have a "better body" (however you define it)—no matter how clean you eat, what workouts you do or how healthy you are on the outside? Or why you feel good for a short time when you do lose those 10 pounds, only to see that nothing in your life has changed?

When we focus on the external alone (our body, money, material items that bring us happiness), we *miss the mark every time—because these things are unable to satisfy our deepest desires.*

Think harder and be honest: *What does losing (or gaining) those 10 pounds really mean to you?*

Speaking for myself, the times I've been happiest and most fulfilled in my outside life, my body has also followed suit.

As in feeling more amazing in my skin than ever before.

As in, actually feeling good in my clothes, in pictures, and at the gym.

As in not worrying so much about my weight or my food or my size— at all (and those thoughts used to dominate my mind or dictate my overall peace in life).

Sure, I am taking care of myself physically—nourishing my body instead of fearing food so much, and moving in ways that bring me joy, but outside of the kitchen and the gym, I am:

- More connected with friends and community
- Praying and reflecting daily
- Seeing the world and new days full of opportunity rather than drudgery
- Pursuing the things I love
- Using my voice more and people pleasing less
- Making time for my favorite hobbies and crafts, like writing
- Loving others well and seeking to be a change I genuinely wish to see in the world
- Feeling less stress
- Getting enough rest and can focus and give my best work when I do work
- Not wasting hours on my social media

It's that whole mind-body connection thing.

Where your mind is, the body will follow, and that, my friend, is the power we must tap into first on our journey to unleashing your body's natural ability to be more intuitive with food, fitness and simply the way you live.

Reflection + Rule Break Project:
Reflect in a journal or bullet journal what the "feeling" of "10 pounds from now" really is and what it means to you. You can list it out or write an essay, whatever you are comfortable with. Just be honest with yourself about why you want to make a change.

Bonus:
Identify at least three other things in your life which can give you "that" feeling you have been correlating to your body size.

Do one of them today. Here are a few examples:

- *Paying it forward*
- *Reaching out to connect with an old friend*
- *Taking 30-60 minutes to "just do you."*
- *Sharing positivity with someone else today*
- *Getting fresh air in nature*
- *Unplugging from social media*
- *Praying for your mind (and body) "Lord, I pray specifically you take me to the weight you want to be"—releasing it up takes a load off!*

Whatever you choose to do, do it because it makes you feel good.

Intuitive Eating, Moving & Living Defined

While feeling good is a must if you want to have a healthy relationship with food, your body, or fitness, this book is about more than just "feeling good" (There are *plenty* of 30-day challenges, beachbody workouts, Instagram bloggers, Dr. Oz segments, 21 day detoxes, calorie counting apps, "clean eating" books, programs, and food **RULES** aimed at helping you do that).

Instead, this is book about *being intuitive.*

What exactly does "being intuitive" mean?

In essence, "being intuitive" is *honoring and trusting your body.*

"Getting back" to the way you were designed to think, feel and know exactly what your body needs, what it wants.

To a degree, being intuitive" IS feeling good because we humans are hardwired to want to feel good and in balance (ie. not too full, not too hungry, energetic, not overworked, etc.). But it is also about so much more than the diet, health and wellness claims.

"Being intuitive" is *not* about rules. Instead, it's about tuning in, inside, to your own body's natural cues and rhythms. And, yes, breaking some rules.

"Being intuitive" is boldness and confidence, knowing that your body wants to work for you, not against you.

Fear is the opposite of intuitiveness.

What does "being intuitive" look like in action?

With food, **intuitive eating** is:

- **Eating when you are hungry** and stopping when you are full.
- Not dwelling or obsessing about food, but using food as fuel and enjoying good bites along the way.
- Not associating food with body rolls, scales or your morals; **you're neither good nor bad** depending on what you eat.
- **Eating real, whole foods** your body recognizes as food and was meant to thrive upon.
- **Listening to your gut.** Learning and understanding what foods sit well with you or don't sit well with you and choosing what to eat based on how food makes you feel (as opposed to self-imposed food rules).
- **Imperfect.** Intuitive eating does not mean you'll always choose the "healthy" or "right" foods. You won't always feel as if we've had a "perfect" balance.
- **Rhythmic.** We feel pleasantly full (but not stuffed) after a meal and pleasantly hungry (but not starving) before the next.
- **Seasonal.** The desire for warming foods in the winter, crisp refreshing foods in the summer, harvested apples in the fall, and fresh greens in the spring.

- **Pleasurable**, delightful, tasty, and energizing.

- Recognizing that **not every meal has to tickle your tastebud**s, but can still nourish your body.

- **Varied**. Meats, fats, fruits, and vegetables, and starches play a role in normal, intuitive eating. You don't restrict your body from the foods it was intended to thrive upon.

- **Feeling good.** Good food in the right amounts and at the right times excites the senses. It provides tactile and taste sensations as we eat, and a pleasurable "full" feeling afterward. When we finish a meal, we feel comforted and renewed - physically, emotionally, and even spiritually.

Intuitive movement is:

- **Moving your body how it was designed to move**, a combination of endurance and aerobic, strength, power, flexibility and restful activities.

- **Lifestyle movement.** Lifting a heavy suitcase, walking to the cafe a few blocks away, running in a game of tag, moving boxes into your new apartment, swinging on the monkey bars, and building your strength to squat twice your bodyweight on the barbell.

- **Honoring the balance of work and rest.** Acknowledging your muscles don't always have the same 100% every day and feeling them recover as your rest.

- **Not obsessively calculating** how many steps you've walked or calories you've burned or whether or not your heart rate is in the "fat-burning" zone.

- **Not chiseling, contorting, or shaping your body to look like someone else.** Using movement to express your energy, vitality, joy and fun.

- **Not forcing yourself** to run 6 miles like you did the two days before if you feel beat down, and resting, walking, doing yoga, sleeping in, or hitting the weights instead.

Intuitive living and thinking are:

- An all-knowing **sense of worth, respect and acceptance** of who you are.

- **Connection** to something or someone greater than yourself (spirituality).

- **Recognition of your unique gifts, talents, strengths, skills and purpose** you have in this world.

- **Pursuing your heart's passions** and doing the things you love.

- **Empathy and awareness** of others outside yourself and attuning to other people around you.

- **Having boundaries for yourself** and not saying "yes," to everything.

- **Not playing negative self-talk** on repeat in your head.

- **Accepting no one else's definition of who you are.**

- **Knowing your *own* truth**, and using that as your guiding light.

Intuitiveness is many of things, but ultimately: Intuitiveness is **<u>CONNECTION</u>** to your body, your mind, and your soul.

Looking at these lists, how have YOU been disconnected from yourself? Think about where you are today, because that will give you some ground work to start working from on your personal journey to reconnecting with your natural born intuition.

Easier said than done? Nah. Not when you keep it simple.

And that is exactly what we're going to do. Starting with "lightbulb" moments.

What Happens When You Eat a Twinkie? My (Intuitive Eating) Lightbulb Moment

Lightbulb Moment: (noun, informal) a moment of sudden inspiration, revelation, or recognition.

"Lightbulb" Moments *are* like "tipping points," turning points and *game changers in how you think.*

When we talk about "breaking the rules," and *changing the game in the way you eat, move, and relate to your body,* a "Lightbulb Moment" (or several) may be in store.

Lightbulb Moments come in all shapes in sizes.

They are that one shining moment in the story where *everything* changes.

- Belle discovers the Beast is her prince.
- Noah hears a message and builds an ark to survive the flood.
- Rudy believes he can make the game winning touchdown.
- David defeats Goliath with a sling shot.
- Your frizzy-haired middle school self discovers the hair straightener.
- We discover the world is not flat.
- Henry Ford invents the Model T.
- Steve Jobs conceptualizes the iPhone.

Without these Lightbulb Moments—a revelation, an epiphany and often change in our thoughts, or behavior—we stay stuck.

A critical Lightbulb Moment for healing my relationship with food and my body came in the form of a Twinkie.

The Twinkie Snack Challenge

"Choose one," she said.

I had three options: Twinkie, Ding-Dong, or Oatmeal Cream Pie.

And I *had* to choose. Afternoon snack challenges were NOT optional in the eating disorder treatment center.

Shuffling my feet down the food line while shaking inside, my thoughts frantically raced— calculating the calories and fat-grams (which of course I knew without looking at the labels), and psyching myself up by saying, *"It will be ok. You will be out of here before long. You can burn it off when you're out."*

Indecisive over the "best" option to select, I just made the sudden decision to reach for the Twinkie, which was a childhood favorite I hadn't eaten in years.

Taking my seat in silence at the dining table, alongside 11 other "inmates" (the other teen girls in my short-term residential treatment home), a hushed silence fell over the crowd. It was as if a black cloud rolled in as we each opened our Hostess plastic cakes and prepared to dig in.

"Fifteen minutes, girls," the recovery coach reminded us.

Fifteen agonizing mandatory minutes to complete our spongy cake snack. If we didn't eat them, there was a Boost or Ensure-Plus Nutritional Shake as backups.

Taking a deep breath in, I begrudgingly sank my teeth into the airy, cream-filled vanilla cake as a sea of sugar, corn syrup, vegetable oil and food additives swarmed into my mouth, igniting my alertness brain receptors and taste-buds. A spiral of disordered food rules and body image jabs ran through the back of my mind: "You are going to get so fat!" "Eww, you're so lazy!" "That's disgusting!"

Slowly chewing the sponge and cringing inside, I coached myself, "Just breathe. It's ok. It's just a Twinkie." This was followed by another slow bite, chewing the spongy vanilla puff and letting the cream melt on my tongue.

Fifteen minutes felt like an agonizing 15 hours. *When would the torture end?*

Finally, finishing the last crumb of my Twinkie, the thoughts only grew louder and a fuzzy feeling of brain fog and digestive bloating set in. I proceeded to sit on the living area sofa, wanting nothing more than to curl up in a ball and cry. I was convinced that I, and my body, were goners—going south to become a lazy, fat, self-ashamed American, as I had feared for the past five years.

And there was nothing I could do about it. There was no StairMaster or running trail in sight, no escaping the watchful eyes of the recovery staff, no "getting back on the bandwagon tomorrow."

And I had a plate full of Shrimp Fettuccini Alfredo coming my way for dinner within a matter of hours.

I felt like a prisoner in my skin.

Until I woke up the next morning, and…

Nothing happened.

The Twinkie was in the rear view mirror and my body didn't balloon up overnight.

My brain fog subsided. My bloating distilled. And my brain was preoccupied now with something else.

So, what happens when you eat a Twinkie?

Lightbulb Moment: **Nothing**.

And what happens when you begin trusting that your body *intuitively knows* how to take care of you (even when a "little dirt" gets in the way)?

Lightbulb Moment: Amazing things.

Beyond Twinkies: Multiple Lightbulb Moments

The art of letting go and listening more to your body (and less to the thoughts or judgements you've concocted in your head) does not happen overnight. Everyone's timeline is completely different, and that is okay.

"Becoming more intuitive" is typically a combination of multiple experiences, trials and errors, epiphanies and tipping points, all helping you realize that your body is smart and **knows *how* to be *intuitive* when you listen to it.**

Your body *wants to work for you*—not against you.

In my own experience, it wouldn't be until approximately ten years after the Twinkie incident that I *finally* began trusting my body for the first time since I was a kid. Multiple little lightbulb "tipping points" along the way taught me more and more that my body totally knew what to do with Twinkies, butter, leafy greens, rest days from workouts and everything in between.

More lightbulbs, epiphanies and experiments paved the way to more trust of and in my body, and more tuning in.

There was the **butter** incident, when I swallowed the lump in my throat and made a choice to cook my greens in a tablespoon of butter in my pan.

Lightbulb Moment: I didn't develop rolls on my belly, I felt satisfied (and my greens tasted really good).

Then there was the **bleacher fight.** Every afternoon for a year straight, I hit the local stadium bleachers—rain or shine—to run up and down stairs for an hour. Until one day, I didn't. I fought every itch and negative comment inside myself because I was tired gosh darn it! And I didn't want to run the bleachers.

Lightbulb Moment: My leg muscle did not instantly turn into cellulite.

Then there was the **Crystal Light experiment**, where I cut Crystal Light out of my diet after realizing the bloating, abdominal cramping, shortness of breath and lightheadedness I experienced daily was somehow connected to the artificially sweetened Strawberry-Orange-Banana pink drink that I consumed by the pitcher at lunch and dinner.

Lightbulb Moment: What I eat impacts *how I feel.*

The **"N" word experiment** was also enlightening. No. N-O. Learning to say "No."

"No" was a foreign word to me in my head-driven self and as a people-pleaser. I no longer wanted to spend 6 to 8 hours per day in a gym. I hit a wall and realized I was missing a heck of a whole lot going on in life (outside the gym). I said, "No," for the first time to my third exercise session of the day, and I said "yes" to other (more important things).

Lightbulb Moment: I *CAN* say "no"…and it's ok. It is completely ok for me to find what is right for ME.

Your Lightbulb Moments

You will have your own lightbulb moments— moments, experiences, people, and resources--that will help guide and shape you in *reconnecting to your heart, head, and body,* a language you once knew like the back of your hand.

Whether you've been....

- **Addicted to sugar.** Constantly craving chocolate or even fruit, no matter how hard you fight it.

- **Fearful of fat** and avoiding oil, butter and anything off of the low-calorie menu like the plague.

- **Choosing what you eat based on what guidelines** your Vegan, Paleo or Vegetarian lifestyle says you should eat more than based on how your body feels.

- Hitting the gym for cardio because you **need to burn x-amount of calories today.**

- Reaching for popcorn and wine **in front of the TV every night.**

- **Eating almond butter straight out of the jar with a spoon,** then looking up and wondering, "What happened?"

- **Hating on your thighs every time you slip your jeans on—** vowing you'll do more squats, and eat fewer carbs.

- **Constantly comparing yourself** to "her" body, her life, or her success—displayed for all to see on Instagram.

You don't have to keep living like a robot.

Enter: Being intuitive. Or as I like to call it, "Breaking the Rules."

Break the Rules: My 3-Step Method for Reawakening Your Intuition

The freedom to eat intuitively, move intuitively and live intuitively will come when you do one thing: *Let go.*

Release your grip on the food and exercise rules, body standards and unrealistic expectations you've been holding on to. Surrender and listen to your body, mind, and soul. And even break some rules.

Like holding a butterfly in a gently open hand, when we let go of our self-imposed rules and our "should" monsters, we allow that butterfly to "fly," experiencing a tremendous, enlightening freedom to simply just....be.

But what happens if you try to hold on tightly to that butterfly? It's crippled and crushed. It's wings are crimped and it can no longer be free.

But how?

Yeah, okay. So the whole "intuitive" thing and "letting" thing sounds good in theory. But...

How do I stop caring and erase the rules?!
How do I stop trying so hard?!
How the heck do I just listen to your body?!

Letting go to "**listen to your body**" and "eat intuitively" goes FAR beyond what another 30-day diet, workout program, or food list can give you.

These methods give you rules to follow and tell you WHAT to do (what checklists to check), but they don't guide or teach you HOW to reawaken your natural-born intuition (the ability you have within you

ALREADY to be totally healthy, full of energy, comfortable in your own skin and confident).

Break the Rules does.

The process of re-awakening your intuition, specifically with food, your body and your mindset, involves recognizing truths such as:

- **All you need to focus on is one meal at a time**— other opportunities to try different foods will be there later.
- **Your body needs and deserves energy to function**. Eating is a natural born human right, not something you have to earn.
- **The gym will still be there tomorrow**. And your muscles will not atrophy is one day.
- **Your body won't gain 5 pounds just because you ate a slice of pizza**. Nor does a number on a scale define you.
- **Your true identity and worth are not found in the size of your jeans**, the number of likes on your Instagram, or your ability to run on a treadmill at 10 miles per hour and eat low carb every day.
- **Your purpose on this earth is about so much more than counting calories**, stepping away on StairMasters, or worrying about what you will or won't eat at the dinner party.

Becoming more intuitive involves reflecting inward. Checking in, and asking yourself: *"How do I feel?" and "What is my truth?"*

Becoming more intuitive also involves **80/20 balance**.

Eighty percent of the time eating real whole foods your body was made to thrive upon (sustainable proteins, fresh colorful veggies, healthy fats), the other 20-percent, "letting life happen." No perfection. Not sweating the small stuff.

80/20 means things like…

- **Eating birthday cake** on your birthday
- **Cooking** fresh homemade real foods most of the time, and occasionally eating out.
- **Not earning your food,** but fueling your body
- **Thinking of food when you're hungry…**and filling your head with other thoughts outside meal time
- **Trying a bite of the cookie** your mom made with her two loving hands (even though you think sweets are bad for you)
- Eating a **salad one day, a burger** the next
- **Loving how green juice or bone broth makes your belly feel!**

Vacations happen. Eating out happens. Birthday parties happen. And guess what: It's ok! Food cannot hurt you.

And lastly, "being intuitive" involves learning how to *trust* your body (again). Not rules.

Three Steps to Break the Rules

To help you easily do this, I've created a simple **3-Step Method** that has worked not only for me, but hundreds of others in my clinical practice over the past several years to find food, body, and mindset freedom, as well as dust the dirt off their naturally-born intuition which they've had deep down, all along.

Unlike other diet programs or self-help books that give you loads of rules, protocols, diet plans, or check boxes to follow, the Method is more of an ongoing natural flow process.

It's something you can continue to come back to time and time again, to work the steps in various ways for any health or lifestyle changes you want to make.

This **3-Step Method entails:**

1. **Gaining Vision:** Getting a clear picture of the healthy, thriving, intuitive version of yourself and the life you want.

2. **Raising Awareness:** Shedding light on any of the lies, stinkin' thinkin,' old habits and myths you've been following or believing, and discovering the truths about food, fitness, your body, your worth to help set you free.

3. **Redefining:** Establishing new healthy habits, lifestyle practices, mindsets, and ways of living your life. Leaving behind your old ways of doing things and moving onwards to creating the new, tangible definition for what "intuitive living" actually means for you.

We've got some heart and head work to do!

The cool thing?

You don't need to worry one bit. All you have to do is follow along and allow **me to lead the way.**

Our journey first begins with **Gaining Vision**: establishing a clear picture of where you are, today. Who your most intuitive, thriving, vibrant self is. And what it is you WANT for yourself in your new life of freedom.

Are *you* really ready to break some rules?

If so, let's go!

Step 1

Gain Vision

Know Where You Are & Where You're Going

"If you can imagine it, it's possible. -Walt Disney"

My phone's battery was at 7%.

And when you're on a road trip in unfamiliar territory, that's basically like saying you're the perfect actor for the movie "Castaway" with no idea where to go or how to get anywhere without your lifeline.

Twenty minutes later, the phone died and there I was, stranded.

Have you ever gone on a road trip without a map or GPS? Maybe traveling across country from New York to California?

Just you, your car, the radio, and the open road.

Chances are if you did, you didn't get very far.

At least, you didn't get anywhere you intended without any navigation or eventually making a plan of some sort, running out of money, or defining the purpose of your trip.

To get anywhere, including becoming more intuitive, free, and pushing past your fears, you've got to know where you're coming from and where you're going (or at least have an idea).

I call this **"Gaining Vision"** and it entails getting a clear picture of **where you are today in your relationship with food and your body, and knowing what it is you want** for your ideal thriving life (where we are going together).

When we are deeply connected to our vision, the ability to be intuitive comes so much easier. We are no longer bound by the rules, old habits or stinkin' thinkin' we've been living by for far too long because we have a direction OUT. We can move in the direction of our dreams and a bigger purpose.

We are better able to use our heart, gut and head as barometers for our daily decisions, from food choices to self-care choices, energy usage, and how we spend our time, walking in the direction of our "dreams".

Your Baseline

A baseline is ground zero. Our starting place.

Before we think about what freedom or "less" self-imposed rules look like, we need to understand where we are at, today.

The pain points,biggest challenges or get-ups you currently face with food, your body and how you see or think about yourself.

Chances are you already know these like the back of your hand.

In my own struggle with food and my body, for instance, I woke up most days with a black cloud looming over my head, just wanting things to be different.

I lived by rules and fears, such as:

- I must complete 1000 crunches before brushing my teeth, getting dressed or eating breakfast

- I can only eat a lean protein source and veggies for lunch
- I *should* choose the low calorie option
- I *should* say "yes" (even though I want to say "no")
- If I don't work out today, I am a lazy bum (and I'll gain body fat)
- Avoid eating out at all costs
- I'm not good enough (and I need to look like X, succeed at Y, and check off Z check box in order to feel good enough)

Anything BUT intuitive.

More like, counter intuitive.

Although I didn't like these rules and "shoulds" I created for myself, I often felt like I had no other options (and I had no idea how NOT to believe them).

Chances are you have your own rules, your shoulds or your own traps too. Sticky places where you feel stuck or in a funk.

Reflection + Rule Break Project:
Think about where you are today. What top rules, shoulds or funks have you been in lately with your body, food, fitness, how you treat or speak to yourself? How have you been "counter-intuitive" lately?

Make a bullet point list of whatever top "pain points" comes to mind. This list will give you some clarity so you can know what you DON'T want.

Need some ideas of funks others have been in? Here are a few:

- Constantly thinking about food or my next meal
- Comparing myself to "that girl"
- Binge eating when I am alone
- Always craving sugar

- Eating the same thing every day
- Food fears
- Food timing rules
- Know how to lose weight or gain weight, but no idea how to maintain
- Weighing myself every day
- Feeling like I don't deserve nice things
- Lack of confidence in my ideas
- Restricting during the day

Once you have a baseline of where you're at, we can then focus on where you're going.

Defining Your Vision

What would intuitive eating, fitness and living mean, or look like for you in an ideal world?

In the last chapter, we defined what it *currently* looks like, and your own definitions of what you *think* it could like. Now we will get more specific.

We are going to define your vision and figure out exactly what you want for your ideal version of "intuitiveness" in all areas—Heart, Gut and Head.

What would it be like if you fully lived in accordance with your heart, body, and mind's natural cues and leadership (no over thinking or second-guessing yourself)?

Gaining Vision involves both imagining and creating a renewed version of healthy, thriving, intuitive you.

I call this **"Putting on Your Belle Dress."**

Put on Your Belle Dress

When I was a little girl, all I wanted to be was Belle from "Beauty & the Beast."

She was brunette and I could identify with her more than red-headed Ariel or blonde Cinderella. She was smart, witty and didn't need a man to define her. My kind of babe!

So, for the Halloween following the movie's summer release, I knew hands down who I wanted to be: Belle.

My mom went to town with the idea. She found a local seamstress who specialized in making children's Halloween costumes, and Party City ate my dust—the seamstress made me my own, customized yellow Belle ballgown.

I don't think I took that thing off for weeks. I wore it most days, just playing dress-up and pretending to be the Belle of the ball.

I wore it to my birthday (costume) party (I am an October baby), school Halloween parade, and the night of Halloween, I remember sitting in the back of my mom's minivan, waving to all my "fans" on the street like Miss America.

I didn't *just* have a Belle dress. I *was* Belle.

The remainder of that 4-year-old year, my Belle dress was my personal "superhero" costume—any time I put it on, I instantly transformed into a Disney princess who could do anything she put her mind to, and who knew she was beautiful both inside and out.

Time went on and more Halloweens rolled around, and I mixed up my attire. Jasmine one year, a hippie, a pajama girl. However, *nothing* ever compared to my beautiful Belle dress—or the way I felt when I wore my ballgown…unstoppable.

Until today.

My Belle dress taught me a mighty powerful lesson. Something that I would tap into years later, when I found myself *really struggling* with my worth, unhealthy habits, and low self-esteem.

The lesson?

As we THINK, therefore we BECOME.

4-year-old me *thought she was Belle*, every time she put on that dress.

So, in turn, I acted like Belle, talked like Belle, thought like Belle and I **became** Belle every time I wore my yellow dress.

The same lesson applies today, concerning WHO YOU WANT TO BE and WHAT YOU WANT YOUR LIFE TO LOOK LIKE.

As you think, therefore you BECOME.

Reflection + Rule Break Project:
Ok—your turn.

Who did you want to be (or be like) as a kid?

A Disney princess? Mary Kate and Ashley Olsen? Wonder Woman?

Fast forward to today…WHO do you want to be? No, not a celebrity now or even your grandma.

Who is the THRIVING, SOUL-ON-FIRE, INTUITIVE-LIV-ING YOU that you want to be?

This picture can look like anything you want.

What does intuitive, thriving you think like? Eat like? Workout like? Treat herself like? Talk like? Act like? Look like?

I want you to gain a really clear picture of WHO healthy, thriving YOU truly is.

Do you...

- Eat when you're hungry - and *know* when you're hungry in the first place?
- Binge or purge—or eat to satisfy and nourish?
- Enjoy not feeling bloated after you eat because you know what foods sit well?
- Order what you want AND what feels good from the menu?
- Define your identity based on not on your diet or food choices (paleo, vegan, vegetarian, etc.), but on your You-niqueness?
- Sleep in and skip your workout sometimes, just because you need the rest?
- Move your body for fun and joy?
- Speak honestly and embrace vulnerability?
- Refrain from judging others because you're confident in your skin?
- Have a deep, spiritual connection?
- Have balance?
- Let the little things stress you out?
- Try to control every situation?
- Have a "healthy" control?
- Waste time or maximize it?
- Find yourself able to be present—or are you constantly worried, thinking about the next thing?
- Cry when you need to?
- Pursue your dream job or are you stuck in the 9-5 you loathe, fearful of leaving security?

Make a list of who this intuitive, thriving, happy, heart-beating YOU is—the girl you want to be. The girl you want to work toward becoming.

After you've finished your list, look at it, and **reflect**:

"As I think, therefore I become."

Even though you may not feel or believe you are her yet—**pretend you are her TODAY.**

Embody her. Make decisions, choices, actions and think like she would—in **all circumstances**. From what you choose to eat and how you nourish your body, to how you speak to yourself, how you dress and carry yourself, what you do with your time, etc.

And, when a decision comes up around "What to do?!" Ask yourself: **WHAT WOULD INTUITIVE ME DO?**

Put on your "Belle Dress" mindset.

A Word on Goal Vomit

The "Putting on your Belle Dress" mindset can seem a lot like goal setting—casting a vision for what you're "going for" in your life.

But it's not.

The thing is, goals can be nauseating. How many goals have you talked about or attempted to set in your life? And how many have you achieved?

In theory, the idea of goals is GREAT. It's always great to be working toward something!

However, the problem that many non-intuitive folks often run into when they focus on *future goals*—what they want three months, five years, or 10 years from now—is that they don't always buy into their goals from the very beginning.

Since following their intuitively-led heart does not come naturally, their gut feelings often lead them astray and their mindset can cast self-doubts or inner-critic jabs, and many folks give up on the idea that their goal is *actually possible* after writing them down.

Enter: the Belle Dress, or the "as if," mindset. Acting AS IF you have already attained or discovered what it is you really want all along.

Goals don't have to start or evolve *tomorrow* or *three months* or *five years from now.* They can happen TODAY.

Instead of saying "tomorrow" or "I am working towards it," the new, more intuitively-connected you start immediately, as you make up your mind to embody "Belle" in the present moment.

In short, no more goal vomit necessary.

Un-clouding Your Vision: 90-Year Old You

Are you struggling to get a "clear picture" of who intuitive you really are or who you could be?

No sweat.

Envision yourself at 90 years old. Grab a pen and paper, and answer this prompt:

"At 90 years old, I want my life to look like…"

Also, consider what you will want to look back on from your life and say about it — how you spent your days? What you cared about? What didn't you care about? How you took care of yourself? Where you spent your time?

If your 90-year-old self were to speak to your current self, what would she say? What advice would she give regarding the way you live your life now and what matters most?

It doesn't have to be a story or a perfectly written piece, you can brain dump it. Jot down anything and everything that comes to mind and use it to gain some perspective.

Get clarity and vision around what you want in your relationship with food, fitness, your body, your self-concept, and how you carry yourself by working backwards, from the top down.

To Infinity & Beyond

Get it? Got it? Good.

Now we're ready to get into the fun stuff—Awakening your intuitive self!

In the remainder of this book, we're going to take a deep dive into *unleashing your* **Intuitive Heart, Intuitive Mind, and Intuitive Body.**

To do that, we will walk through the rest of the **3-Step Method:**

Step 2: Raising Awareness. Recognizing lies, myths, beliefs and stinkin' thinkin that have shaped your current intuition (or lack thereof). We will also explore new truths about what having an Intuitive Heart, Mind and Body actually mean.

Then, we move on to Step 3: Redefine: rewriting your intuition story and reawakening your ability to be intuitive within your Heart, Mind, and Gut as we discuss 13 Habits Intuitive People Do. I will also give you an Intuitive Blueprint, which is a personal roadmap or plans to begin implementing more intuitiveness in each of these areas as well.

Ultimately, remember, this 3-step Method is about guiding you HOW to trust your body and letting go.

Step 2

Raise Awareness

"Knowledge is power"

In order to transform your life, you must first transform your mind.

That's exactly what Step 2, "Raising Awareness," in our 3-Step Method (to reconnect to your own intuition) is all about. Recognizing any old lies, myths, beliefs and mindsets keeping you stuck (non-intuitive), and covering your mind (and your heart and body) with new truths.

When you realize the misguided (false) "truths" you've been believing about yourself, food, and your body, it makes "listening to your body" and "being intuitive" a no-brainer.

Where to start?

From the inside out. The deepest part of you, your Intuitive Heart. Raising awareness to WHO you are. Your intuitive self *at your core.*

Then we move on to your Intuitive Mind. Your thoughts, beliefs and potentially misguided rules you've made for yourself. And lastly, your Intuitive Body. Your connection to your food, your gut, fitness, weight and everything in between.

Although it may sound odd to talk about your heart or your mindset in a book about intuitive eating, exercise and body image, we must begin understanding ourselves FIRST.

In fact, often times any struggles we have with food, food rules, "bad habits," disordered eating and poor body image are not about the food, our jean size or number on a scale at all.

So let's raise awareness to who you are. Your bad-ass intuitive self. That girl you were born to be, and that girl you may have become disconnected with.

Things like, how you like your eggs...

Part 1: Your Intuitive Heart

In the movie, "Runaway Bride," Julia Roberts plays repeat bride-run-way offender Maggie Carpenter, who continues to have a number of unsuccessful relationships out of her FEAR of being married. Throughout the film, we witness Maggie fall in love, ring the wedding bells, then run away. Every single time.

An interesting quirk highlighted in the film also depicts Maggie's odd interests. Her tastes continually change. Depending the man on her arm, Maggie is a chameleon--to his likes and interests, including how he likes his eggs.

"Over easy." *Me too.*
"Poached." *Me too.*
"Scrambled." *Me too.*

Maggie *never* knows how she likes her own eggs, *until*, she meets bachelor "Ike" (Richard Gere), a *New York Times* journalist, sent to write a story on the "Runaway Bride" and things change.

As you can guess, the more Maggie gets to know inquisitive Ike, the more she discovers who she is (her intuitive self). Her love fears fade. She begins pursuing her true passions. **And** she discovers how she likes her eggs (Benedict).

Voila!

The more you get to know yourself (your Intuitive Heart) the MORE natural "being intuitive" (with ANYTHING) becomes.

Who You Are

Who am I?

It's a question we've all asked ourselves at one time or another, dating back to our middle school braceface days.

In fact, I'll never forget the day I got braces.

A few weeks earlier, my orthodontist told me my retainer would no longer help fix my overbite and forced me to become a metal mouth for *at least* nine long months. Hearing this harsh reality, I psyched myself up for the long nine month road ahead:

"It won't be that bad…"

"Tons of kids get braces all the time…"

However, come D-day, with my high school's blue and gold colors slapped on my teeth, I looked in the mirror to smile and…burst into tears.

That's not me—really?!

Self-conscious already about the bump on my nose (just like my dad's), my wavy brown (not straight and blonde) hair, and knock-off Doc Martin's on my feet, braces on my teeth were the straw that broke the camel's back.

It couldn't be me, could it?

Ugly. Fat. Stupid. I thought in my head.

And, in my heart of hearts, the last thing I felt connected to was...me. All I wanted to be—and look like—was anyone else BUT me.

Long story short, I made it through those long nine months and I lived to tell about it. But deep down inside, I wanted nothing to do with being me.

It took me another 10 years before I started waking up to the fact that my body shape, my weight, the "weaknesses" or flaws I saw in myself, and my braces did not (and do not) define me.

It was not until I began to get to know Lauryn—the real Lauryn—at my core, and realize that there was only ONE me on this planet, that I began to feel more *connected to her* in my heart.

The same thing goes for you.

Do you want to get more "connected" to yourself? Become a more intuitive eater? Move or work out based on how you feel rather than rituals or rules? Able to listen and lead your life with your heart, gut, and mind instead of jumping through hoops, trying to control things out of anxiety, people-pleasing, or "shoulding" yourself all the time?

It all begins with your **Intuitive Heart**: Knowing in your core *who you are*—your identity, character strengths and personality, gifts and abilities, passions, values, life mission and purpose.

Daddy's 10 Questions for Life

As a kid, I was a total "daddy's girl."

One of my fondest memories of my father is his "Daddy's 10 Questions for Life" he asked me every night as he tucked me in and I lay my head down on my pillow to rest.

They went something like this:

1. Do you know that you are special?
2. Do you know that God has blessed you?
3. Do you know that you can grow up and be anything you want to be?
4. What does Daddy want you to be? (Happy!)
5. Do you know that you should be a leader and respect yourself?
6. Do you know that you should learn to love the truth?
7. Do you know you should be fair and try to do the right thing?
8. Do you know that you should have a positive attitude and look for the best in others?
9. Do you know you should be kind and reach out to others in need?
10. Do you know you should be a good friend and cherish your friendships?

Affirming, don't you think?

My dad did an excellent job of letting me know my own worth.

However, while Dad was one of my #1 fans growing up (and I was his), I did not always see my own value and worth the way he (or others) saw it.

Pop quiz: Why is it that we are so easily able to see the goodness, value, strengths and "best" in others—but so rarely see it ourselves?

Answer: Because we aren't convinced of our own worth.

Think about some successful people in life—

- Michael Phelps, an Olympic record-holding swimmer.
- Julia Roberts, a Hollywood starlet.
- Beyonce Knowles or Taylor Swift—music divas.

- Abraham Lincoln—president, who lost 15 elections before becoming our 16th President.
- Michael Jordan—"the greatest basketball player of all time."

What makes these people, not just good, but **great** and successful?

Answer: **They know who they are.**

They have a clear vision and profound understanding of their character **strengths, personality, gifts, talents, passions,** and **values**—all that propel them to live out their life **purpose,** no questions asked, and be great at their craft.

You don't see Michael Jordan calling himself an "actor," even though he's been in some commercials and movies. You don't see Julia Roberts on stage belting out lyrics, even though she broke out in karaoke songs in the movie "My Best Friend's Wedding."

The cool thing? No one else on this planet has what you (or Michael Jordan or Julia Roberts) have to offer.

Just like no two fingerprints or snowflakes are alike, there is NO ONE on this earth who is exactly like you and life would be completely boring if there were!

Plus, for the record: The original version of anything are worth far more than copies.

Take Vincent VanGogh's "Starry Night" painting, for instance. We've seen dozens of versions of this painting in our lifetimes—from history textbooks, to desktop backdrops, quilts, and household wall art replicas. But not one of these copies compares to the actual famous "Starry Night" painting, housed in New York's Museum of Modern Art. You, my friend, are an original.

Unfortunately, many of us spend our lives and thoughts, focusing on the things about ourselves we want to change or improve, or we waste our energy on comparing ourselves to others who seemingly have better lives, hotter bodies, cuter clothes or more likes on social media than us.

Similar to what happens when we hear nine positive feedback statements, and one negative—we focus on the negative or critical comment. The same thing happens with the way we see ourselves.

Clear the blinders by identifying your unique form—who you were created to be.

In our lives, our **function** (our purpose, what we are created to do), always follows our **form.** Your life will be most effective, purpose-filled and *intuitive* (connected and free), when you first recognize your **form** (your natural **strengths, personality, gifts, and passions).**

Then, you align your **form with your personal values and purpose,** the dreams you go after, what matters most to you, and how you spend your time, focus and energy.

Bonus: Once you know your true **form**—and begin embracing her— the daily little "intuitive" decisions, which once seemed like such a big deal, become easy-peasy lemon squeezy.

- How do you like your eggs? Scrambled.
- Should you take this job? No. I hate sitting at desks all day.
- Running or weight training? Running breaks my body down. Weight training makes me feel strong and builds my body up.
- Do you want fries with that? Not really. They hurt my tummy and I don't feel like the most thriving version of myself when I don't feel well.
- Should you donate to that charity? Yes! I totally believe in that mission.

Ah. Intuitive living made simple.

Scratching your head about *who this* **best version of you is—your form—to begin living out of your true, intuitive self?**

Let's get to know *you* a little bit better.

Rain Puddles, Forts & Mud Pies

Whenever I first start working with an individual on answering that million-dollar question of "Who are you?" and connecting back to their most-intuitive and natural self, I always first ask: **Who were you as a kid?**

That answer often comes much easier.

Little kids are experts in being intuitive and 100% themselves before any of the middle school mean girls, Abercrombie & Fitch designer dud contests, SnapChat, A-plus spelling test pressure, and junior high Sadie Hawkins' dances set in.

Think about it. As a kid:

1. What strengths or positive character traits did you have?
2. What skills or talents came naturally to you?
3. What 3-5 things did you love to do with your time?
4. What interested you in school, in play, in your home life, and in friendships?
5. What did you say you wanted to be when you grew up?
6. What memorable teachers, mentors, lessons or experiences were positive influences in your life? How so? List 3-5.

You are still that same person you were.

Even though you've had tons of experiences, people and lessons which have influenced your life and shaped you since then, deep down inside, your unique strengths, personality traits, gifts, and passions have been part of your life since you were a wee little one.

Chew on these answers as we fast-forward to who you are *today* and we uncover the key essentials about your "intuitive" (natural born) self, including: your **strengths** and **abilities**, your **passions,** your **values** and your **purpose**.

Super Powers: Your Strengths

Your character **strengths** are **positive** traits and attributes. They are your superpowers. They are a part of your personality, and are the traits that bring about excellence in your life.

Your character strengths allow you to be the most **thriving** version of yourself when used.

Like personality-finding, strengths tests are a dime a dozen, so I typically start with personal-reflection and mirror-reflection to keep things simple—checking in both with yourself and with others to identify your own strengths.

Step 1: Self-Reflection
Ask yourself these four questions:

1. Think back to your younger self: What top 3-5 character strengths did you possess as a kid?

2. What character traits come naturally to you without thinking about it? Some examples are: I tend to think about others. I like the truth. I am super determined. (See "Strengths Finder 2.0 Strengths" in the following pages for inspiration.)

3. What do you do differently than other people?

4. When do you get most passionate or energized around what you're doing?

Step 2: Mirror-Reflection

Asking others what they see in us can help us remove our rose-colored glasses when it comes to how we see ourselves.

Email, call or text 3-5 different individuals you are close to you, and ask what qualities they see as your personal strengths.

Ask these people if they could write a story or a reflection about a time you when you were at your best.

Once the feedback arrives, look for the common themes that appear in multiple stories. Make a list of the themes, the key examples that support each them, and what they suggest about your strengths. Then using this information, write out a brief profile of who you are when you're at your best.

Uncovering Your Character Strengths

Interested in an idea of what some strengths are? Clifton's Strengths Finder 2.0 is a great resource and strength assessment that identifies 34 character strengths that people may possess. See the Resources section at the end of this book or take the test now at: http://www.strengths-finder.com.

Other popular tests include:
The Enneagram https://www.enneagraminstitute.com
VIA Character Strengths http://www.viacharacter.org
Myer Briggs Personality Test http://www.myersbriggs.org

A Word on Weaknesses
In our weakness, we are made strong.

We tend to consider weaknesses as "bad" parts of ourselves we want to cover up and strengths as "good", however there are times when our weaknesses actually make us stronger.

For instance, my own "weaknesses" of being a people-pleaser and overachiever do have some POSITIVE to them.

As a people-pleaser, I am naturally more caring and considerate of other people. And as an overachiever, I get things done.

It is only when these tendencies hijack my self-care, self concept, or balance that they become detrimental to me and my well-being.

When we talk about strengths and weaknesses regarding our abilities: **Strengths are not necessarily what you're good at, and weaknesses are not what you're bad at.**

We've been raised to believe that our strengths only **equal the success we achieve.** Although "strength" can be related to success, if that's all it is then **a strength is simply the same as performance.**

For instance, like most people, you have some activities or tasks you do well, but hate doing. You have the ability and you can do it. **You just wish you never had to do it again, because it drains you.**

Such activities are not strengths. **They are weaknesses**—you hate them, they detract from you being fully thriving you.

The simplest and best definition of a strength is "an activity that strengthens you." And the correct definition of a weakness is "an activity that weakens you" — even if you're good at it.

And weaknesses are not bad things. "Weak" personality traits can be part of our strengths, and "weak" abilities are simply gifts we have which do not energize us.

Your You-nique Abilities

We have different gifts, according to the grace given to each of us-Romans 12:6

Each of us has gifts and abilities we have discovered and learned over our lifetime. In fact, most people have upwards of 500 to 800 *different* abilities—from building, to leadership, counseling, analytical thinking, organizing, decorating, designing, directing, welcoming, writing, and more!

Like your personality and character strengths, your unique gifts and abilities play into your bigger life purpose—how you use those gifts in this world.

As a lump sum, I call this your **You-nique Ability.**

Your **You-nique Ability** is defined as **what you love to do** and **what you do very well**—then maximizing these in your life, along with your unique personality and character strengths.

Your **You-nique Ability** consists of four parts:

1. **Standout Ability:** Something others notice about you and brings value to others.
2. **Vigor:** That which energizes you and others around you.
3. **Passion:** An ability or skill you love and find yourself using it as often as possible.
4. **Refinement:** A skill, ability or talent you are continually improving, refining and working on—something you're always looking to refine.

When you focus on your You-nique Ability—the gifts, energy, and abilities that come naturally for you—intuitive living REALLY unfolds!

For instance, I have a You-nique Ability with vigor, to ***connect with people.***

People energize me. Encouraging others energizes me. I am a fabulous question-asker. Incredibly interested in other people. And constantly refining this craft in my interactions and work with others.

I also have a You-nique Ability in passion, to write. Words and I connect and flow.

I know writing is my zen, and while some people may find themselves at a loss for words when they pick up a pen and paper (or keyboard), the words flow for me (sometimes too much).

You-nique Abilities can be both activities and hands-on skills, or natural "superpowers" and strengths that *compliment* your character strengths.

You may be You-niquely gifted at design (skill). Perhaps you have a creative, designer's eye and you're great at putting things together.

You could be You-niquely gifted at "reading people" (a superpower), complimenting your character strengths for Connectedness.

Getting clear on your You-nique Abilities will help you connect to your passions, which help you get out of your head or unstuck from any rut.

Thrive Project:
Work the steps to gain clarity on your You-nique Abilities.

Reflection & Rule Break Project:

1. **What activities give you energy, purpose, and passion?** Where do you truly excel?

2. **What do others often say you're good at, ask you advice about, or notice you're a 'natural' at?** Look back on your Character Strengths Reflection, or ask 3 or 4 of your closest friends and family.

3. **What activities, skills, or abilities do you find yourself drawn to time and time again?** There are things you do whether or not you're paid or if others notice.

4. **Make a list of the habits you do on a daily or weekly basis** which produce your best results or allow you to express your

You-nique Abilities. These are typically habits that you've developed over a lifetime. Write them down and choose the ones that are most reflective of your uniqueness and strengths

> *For example*, I start each day with my Daily Devotional and prayer, a habit which totally energizes my strengths to love and serve others well.

5. **Answer this:** "My You-nique Abilities and superpowers are

   _____.

6. **Imagine your You-nique Ability future.** Imagine yourself in a future where you are spending 100% of your time using your You-nique Ability. How would you feel? What would you accomplish? How would your life be different than it is today? Visualizing your "Unique Ability future" inspires confidence and passion.

Need some inspiration? Use this hit list adapted from Rick Warren's SHAPE Assessment to get your wheels turning.

☐ Adapting – The ability to adjust, change, alter, modify
☐ Administrating – The ability to govern, run, rule
☐ Analyzing – The ability to examine, investigate, probe, evaluate
☐ Building – The ability to construct, make, assemble
☐ Coaching – The ability to prepare, instruct, train, equip, develop
☐ Communicating – The ability to share, convey, impart
☐ Competing – The ability to contend, win, battle
☐ Computing – The ability to add, estimate, total, calculate
☐ Connecting – The ability to link together, involve, relate
☐ Consulting – The ability to advise, discuss, confer
☐ Cooking – The ability to prepare, serve, feed, cater
☐ Coordination – The ability to organize, match, harmonize
☐ Counseling – The ability to guide, advise, support, listen, care for
☐ Decorating – The ability to beautify, enhance, adorn
☐ Designing – The ability to draw, create, picture, outline
☐ Developing – The ability to expand, grow, advance, increase
☐ Directing – The ability to aim, oversee, manage, supervise

- ☐ Editing – The ability to correct, amend, alter, improve
- ☐ Encouraging – The ability to cheer, inspire, support
- ☐ Engineering – The ability to construct, design, plan
- ☐ Excelling – The ability to be the best, setting and attaining the highest standard
- ☐ Facilitating – The ability to help, aid, assist, make possible
- ☐ Forecasting – The ability to predict, calculate, see trends, patterns, and themes
- ☐ Implementing – The ability to apply, execute, make happen
- ☐ Improving – The ability to better, enhance, further, enrich
- ☐ Influencing – The ability to affect, sway, shape, change
- ☐ Landscaping – The ability to garden, plant, improve
- ☐ Leading – The ability to pave the way, direct, excel, win
- ☐ Learning – The ability to study, gather, understand, improve, expand self
- ☐ Managing – The ability to run, handle, oversee
- ☐ Mentoring – The ability to advise, guide, teach
- ☐ Motivating – The ability to provoke, induce, prompt
- ☐ Negotiating – The ability to discuss, consult, settle
- ☐ Operating – The ability to run mechanical or technical things
- ☐ Organizing – The ability to simplify, arrange, fix, classify, coordinate
- ☐ Performing – The ability to sing, speak, dance, play an instrument, act out
- ☐ Persevering – The ability to see things to completion, persisting at something until it is finished
- ☐ Pioneering – The ability to bring about something new, groundbreaking, original
- ☐ Planning – The ability to arrange, map out, prepare
- ☐ Promoting – The ability to sell, sponsor, endorse, showcase
- ☐ Recruiting – The ability to draft, enlist, hire, engage
- ☐ Repairing – The ability to fix, mend, restore, heal
- ☐ Researching – The ability to seek, gather, examine, study
- ☐ Resourcing – The ability to furnish, provide, deliver
- ☐ Serving – The ability to help, assist, fulfill
- ☐ Shopping – The ability to collect, or obtain things, getting the highest quality for the best price
- ☐ Strategizing – The ability to think ahead, calculate, scheme
- ☐ Teaching – The ability to interpret, decode, explain, speak

☐ Traveling – The ability to journey, visit, explore

☐ Visualizing – The ability to picture, imagine, envision, dream, conceptualize

☐ Welcoming – The ability to entertain, greet, embrace, make comfortable

☐ Writing – The ability to compose, create, record

On Fire: Your Passions

Your Passions are similar to your Abilities in that they are broad and unique to you, however Passions are *not* necessarily confined to skills.

Instead, your **Passions are your heart's loves that make you YOU— things you love to do, spend your time on, and think about.**

You have interests, hobbies, skills, talents, dreams, and interests that are 100% unique to you, and if and when you don't "feed" these aspects of you, then you, start to starve a piece of your heart. Passions are limitless, and can range from working with children, to painting, photography, rock climbing, nature, writing, volunteering, socializing, and more.

Every day we have a choice as to where we pour our energy, time, and hearts and the paths we pursue.

Where are you spending your energy, your time, and your heart?

In the movie, "The Legend of Bagger Vance," golf caddy Bagger Vance says this to the golfer:

"Inside each and every one of us is one true authentic swing. Something we were born with. Something that's ours and ours alone. Something that can't be taught to you or learned. Something that got to be remembered."

What is that something for you—something you don't have to think twice about, something that comes naturally?

When you cannot think of yours, then you are not connected to your passions. Once you discover the things that make you tick and get excited, you will find that the happiness and passion explode from within.

So, what are your passions?

Reflections & Rule Break Project:

1. Think back on your life, and remember things you wanted to be, the habits you developed naturally, the games you played, the books you read, and see how they may apply to your life and career today.

2. Think of someone who has made a positive difference in your life. What qualities does that person have that you would like to develop?

3. If a 6-inch steel beam was placed across two skyscrapers, for what would you be willing to cross it for? $1000? A million dollars? Your pet? Your brother? Fame? Think carefully.

4. Describe a time when you were deeply inspired.

5. List 10 things you love to do—it could be singing, dancing, magazine reading, drawing, daydreaming, running, anything you love!

6. Five years from now, your local newspaper wants to interview three people close to you: a parent, a sibling, and a friend. What would you want them to say about you?

Still not sure? Here is a list of different hobbies, interests and passions to jog your imagination. Circle the hobbies or interests that appeal to you, then, set an intention to try one this week:

Home & Lifestyle

- Animals/Pets
- Health & Nutrition
- Homemaking
- Cooking
- Baking
- Collecting
- Decorating
- Gardening
- Yardwork
- Sewing/needle work
- Mending/repair
- Woodwork
- Cosmetology/Hairstyling
- Faith-related Activities
- Meditation
- Organizing
- Personal Assisting
- Traveling
- Shopping

Games

- Bingo
- Bunko
- Video games
- Pool
- Board and card games
- Puzzles

Nature

- Bird watching
- Wildlife
  Hiking

- Exploring
- Camping
- Rock Climbing
- Mountain Biking
- Rock Collecting
- Geo-Mapping

Learning, Arts & Creativity

- Acting
- Art collecting
- Antiquing
- Attending plays
- Blogging
- Courses/Adult Education
- Crafting
- Drawing
- Foreign languages
- Leatherworking
- Painting
- Photography
- Pottery
- Designing
- Graphic design
- Fashion
- Museums
- Singing
- School
- Tutoring
- Philosophy
- Reading
- Web design
- Writing
- Toastmasters

Media

- Watching movies
- Going to see movies
- Netflix
- Listening to music
- Listening to podcasts
- Social media
- Reading blogs
- TV

Social Connection

- Community Service/Volunteering
- Bars/Clubs
- Concerts
- Music festivals
- Social clubs
- Dating
- Mentoring
- Meet-up groups
- Book clubs
- Junior League
- Eating out
- Live music
- Church activities
- Holiday activities
- Travel groups
- Politics
- Attending or giving Speeches/Lectures

Fitness & Outdoors

- Biking
- Boating
- Bodybuilding

- Bootcamp
- Bowling
- Boxing/Kickboxing
- Camping
- Climbing
- Cycling/Spinning
- CrossFit
- Dancing
- Fishing
- Football
- Golf
- Hiking
- Hunting
- Horse Riding
- Hockey
- Lacrosse
- Marathons
- Martial Arts
- Obstacle Courses
- Pilates
- Soccer
- Swimming
- Tennis
- Triathlons
- Volleyball
- Walking
- Weight Lifting
- Yoga

Things That Matter: Your Values

Value: (noun): the regard that something is held to deserve; the importance, worth, or usefulness of something.

What makes something valuable?

As a kid, $5 from the tooth fairy was pretty valuable in your eyes until you found out your best friend got $20 from the tooth fairy!

When you shop at TJMaxx and see the former price tag of $150 marked down to $60 on a pair of jeans, you think you're getting top value. Until you see the same jeans somewhere else for $20.

If you booked a coach ticket on American Airlines and all of a sudden were upgraded to first class? Score! Value! Even though it was only due to an underbooked flight.

Really into Pinterest and recipe blogging? Well, meeting your favorite top blogger at a conference makes you go "celebrity crazy"—but your dad wouldn't care less or even know who that is.

Value is in the eye (and mind) of the beholder.

It is how we THINK and what we PERCEIVE to have merit and worth.

And our values—our life values—are the morals, inner compasses, deeply rooted beliefs, convictions, and qualities which we hold near and dear to our heart. They are the values which determine how we live and lead our daily life. They are like our own personal Bill of Rights—your "non-negotiables."

Some examples may include: "I value…

- Doing what I love and loving what I do, no matter what.
- Speaking up for myself.
- Not people pleasing—as hard as it is.
- Not being perfect.
- Being able to have fun.
- Laughter.
- Time spent with others.
- Leaving an impact on young girls.
- Working hard and doing my absolute best.

The answers are limitless and are similar to your own personal "Bill of Rights"—the non-negotiables that allow you to lead a fulfilling life.

Determine your values that define what you most value in your life, your career, your relationships, the way you spend your time, and the impact you want to leave in this world.

Reflections & Rule Break Project:

List 5 to 10 values of yours. Start each with "I value..."

1.

2.

3.

4.

5.

6.

7.

8.

9.

10.

On a Mission: Your Purpose

"What on earth am I here for?"

Figuring out your purpose and mission in life is easier said than done.

However, without a clear purpose or mission, it is easy to get distracted by non-essential to-dos, tasks, goals, or time wasters—including fad diets, diet dogmas, comparison to others, and people-pleasing—rather than doing what you need to do to fully realize your vision and achieve your goals.

So how do *you find your purpose?*

I'm a firm believer that our personal life experiences, trials and tribulations, unique talents and/or interests, all shape us and help us define our personal purposes and missions.

For instance:

- Maybe you were diagnosed with Type I Diabetes at a young age, and today, your mission is to educate kids and parents on coping with the disease.
- Or perhaps you grew up poor and are a first-generation college student. You've known what it's like to live for months at a time with no electricity in your house because your parents couldn't pay the bills. Today, your purpose is to positively impact the lives of other poverty-stricken kids.
- Maybe you discovered self-confidence through physical fitness 10 years ago and transformed your health and your lifestyle from apathetic, office-space desk jockey and couch potato, to a career you LOVE and a life you're excited about.
- Perhaps you are a gifted artist, painting since age 2. Your passion and mission are to do what it is you were made to do: PAINT, and inspire others to find their inner creativity.

The list is endless.

My personal purpose is to help other women find freedom with health, their body, food, and fitness, strengthen their mindsets, and help them become the most optimal version of themselves so they can do the things in this life they were really meant to do—thrive.

A big part of this purpose is rooted in my own identity and relationship with the Lord—my spiritual walk—and who God says I am. I am "fearfully and wonderfully made" and redeemed to be set free. My personal purpose is to be God's hands and feet to those around me and to live the life of freedom, knowing He has set me free.

This purpose came straight from my own experience in healing, recovering my health, life and mind after years spent feeling stuck, unwell and hopeless, doing anything but thriving.

Your **Purpose** is a byproduct and a combination of your history and experiences, your personality, character strengths, your You-nique Abilities, passions, and values.

We've done a great deal of deep work together to build a **solid** foundation for knowing **who you are at your core.**

Describe your purpose below. Try to keep it to 1-3 sentences and don't worry about it being perfect, it will change and evolve as you get to know yourself better.

My purpose is:

_____

_____

_____

Bonus: Feel a little stuck on your purpose?

If you struggle (like I did) with finding your "purpose statement," and need a little more direction, try this 3-part exercise. All you need is a pen and paper.

- Start with your overarching biggest vision. Write a **one-page** summary of what it is you do and what you're passionate about doing.
- Now, take what you wrote and filter it down to a **single paragraph**—no more than 3-5 sentences in length.
- Finally, cut down what you wrote one more time—to just one sentence. This may take several tries!

Recommended Reading for more direction on purpose: *"The Purpose Driven Life"* by Rick Warren and *"Designing Your Life"* by Bill Burnett and Dave Evans.

Part 2: The Power of Your Intuitive Mind

We've already addressed the heart, now let's dig into the power of your mind for helping you reconnect to your natural-born intuition. The mindset that once knew what you wanted, what your body needed and how to love and care for yourself appropriately.

Beyond Self-Help Books

Do you remember....

As a kid, you weren't so hard on yourself, nor did you over think or question your own heart and body's cues.

- You did things you loved.
- You ate when you were hungry and stopped when you were full.

- You spoke your mind.

- You didn't second guess it when your body wanted to run, when it wanted to rest, when it wanted to eat, when it wanted to sleep.

- You didn't calculate every calorie you ate—or the ones you'd be eating later.

- You didn't daydream about chocolate or shame yourself for eating a homemade chocolate chip cookie.

- You voiced your needs when you needed them. You didn't keep them to yourself.

Then, something happened. Your mind got in the way.

- You learned social skills and cultural norms (which are not always a bad thing)
- You began to question if you were really hungry or full.

- You read an article in a magazine or in a blog that told you the "truths" for changing your body.

- You began to wonder if others like you—and what you should do to gain acceptance.

- You compared yourself to other girls who were "prettier" or "thinner" than you.

That mind of yours is a powerful weapon and can be used both for good, like a healthy, empowered, connected relationship with your heart, your body, and food and fitness, or it can be used for not-so-good, such as self-sabotage, stinkin' thinking, questioning yourself, and disconnect from your intuition.

Today marks the day to reconnect with your little-kid intuition, or your "Belle Dress mindset" and be the thriving you you want to be (and the thoughts that set her free), including: the myths and truths you believe, the way you speak to and treat yourself, and no second-guessing your own intuition

Disclaimer: It didn't take overnight to get where you are today (disconnected from an empowered, intuitive mindset), and chances are your mindset played a critical role in the development of many of the current thought patterns and habits you have today.

Thus, "changing your mind" is not simple or an overnight change either. It takes active thought and effort—much like building muscle in the gym.

You won't see strength gains unless you *stay consistent* with a lifting and eating schedule which supports your goals to squat 200 pounds, and you will NOT see a changed or an "empowered" mindset, unless you stay consistent with:

- **Fueling your mind** with truth, positive influences and thoughts
- **Raising awareness** to the lies you've been believing
- **Rewiring** a new language, beliefs and perspectives in your brain

You can read all the self-help books in the world, but all of that information is useless until it is ***implemented***—putting all those insights and information to good use. So let's hop to it!

Know Your Truth

There is **truth in light.** Knowing your truth is an excellent place to begin when transforming your mind. Without truth to counter any lies, second-guessing yourself, and negative mindset ruts you've had, then reconnecting to your naturally-born positive intuitive mindset is going to be an uphill battle.

So what is YOUR truth?

In my final stint in eating disorder recovery treatment "knowing my truth" became a theme and battle cry during my year spent in intensive therapy, groups and soul-searching.

My therapist challenged me to cling to my truth—and know what my truth was (my true healthy recovered self, and my true personal heart-connection to my spiritual, purpose-filled life) in order to overcome the lies and make decisions when options seemed gray.

Exhibit A: Looking in the mirror
Old Mindset Lauryn: "*You are so ugly, fat and stupid.*"
New Mindset Lauryn: "*This is my body. I LOVE and accept it just as I am. You are also fearfully and wonderfully made—a Masterpiece and original. Carbon copies are far less valuable than originals.*"

Exhibit B: Stepping on the scale
Old Mindset Lauryn: "*When you lose 10 pounds, then you'll be beautiful.*"
New Mindset Lauryn: "*You are not a number And you've been telling yourself this same thing—no matter what number you are!*"

Exhibit C: Choosing what to order from the menu
Old Mindset Lauryn: "*I wonder how many calories are in the chicken dish? I must look for the lowest calorie option.*"
New Mindset Lauryn: "*What sounds good, body and gut?*"

Truths set us free—from lies, gray areas, our inner mean girl and the stories (that we tell ourselves).

Facing Your Inner Mean Girl

"Raise your hand if you have ever been personally victimized by Regina George." - *Mean Girls (movie)*

Oh boy. Pull out your boxing gloves. We have some business to do.

As you get to know yourself, or rather, re-meet yourself (Intuitive Heart) and your true identity that may have been quieted for years, chances are you are *also* beginning to recognize some voices that *don't* sound like your own—your inner mean girl or inner critic. Specifically, **how you speak to and treat yourself.**

How we speak to and treat ourselves has a direct impact not only on how to view ourselves, but also our abilities to **think intuitively— connected and driven by our truth.**

For 15 years, I looked in the mirror every day and verbally sais aloud, "You are ugly, fat and stupid!" I even physically slapped myself in the face, stomach, thighs, arms—all this began as a 9 and 10-year-old girl.

With such harsh words, how do you think I viewed and thought of myself? And how do you think that played out in my life?

I hated what I looked like. I also hated who I was on the *inside*. I *believed* I was "nerdy" and a teacher's pet. Not as pretty, popular, or well-liked as the most popular girls in school. I was driven to be perfect—and never felt like I could measure up to my ideals.

In turn, I walked with my head down, totally self-conscious. I constantly checked my mascara or hair in the mirror between classes. I always felt like others were judging me. I spent over an hour getting ready every morning for school, and prayed most days I would get to sit at the cool kid's table at lunch. **I was completely, 100% a classic example of insecurity, and was completely disconnected with my intuition—any ability to be connected to my heart and my head.**

Instead, I was worried about what I should do, who I should be, and who I should please. My inner mean girl only kept things going.

I'm sure you know her, too: Your inner mean girl (i.e. inner critic). That girl who is always hardest on you. That girl who cuts you down, or throws a one-two jab and right hook at you based on:

- What you look like
- What you weigh
- What you wear
- How many Likes you got on your Instagram
- Your status
- Your job
- Your relationships and social life
- Your education
- Your "story"
- And on and on

And, chances are, that that girl—that inner critic—has been with you a very long time.

Personally, my "inner critic" has been with me for as long as I can remember, from 4 years old, to be exact. I was getting dressed for school and I was a fashion diva. I liked things to match and I had my own sense of style. Even at age 4, I was no stranger to wanting to fit in, be accepted and perfect. To say the least, my inner critic (i.e. mean girl) was very vocal, often saying things like *"You're ugly!"* and *"You don't match!"* and *"No one is going to like you!"*

Fast forward to 1st grade—6-years-old, same song, different tune. *"You're never going to get it (how to tell time on a clock)!"* and *"You need to make perfect grades!"* and *"Matt won't like you if you aren't pretty!"* Seriously—in the 1st grade!

Third grade was no different. 8 years old and in dance class. Pink tights, tutus, and a little 3rd grade pre-adolescence tummy. *"You are bigger than the other girls!"* and *"Ew, you're so fat!"*

And the beat went on that way for years. Even today, although far removed from the self-imposed hate of my eating disorder lifestyle, I still catch that inner critic coming out sometimes. Most often saying the phrase, *"You're not good enough"*—whatever the scenario.

Can you relate? Now that we've identified some **truths** about who you are and your Intuitive Heart, now it's time to begin identifying the lies you may have believed about **yourself, which may be holding you back from being who you truly are without second-guessing yourself, thinking positively, and trusting your intuition.**

Reflection & Exercises:

What messages does your "inner mean girl" tell you? It's time to catch them, dead in their traps. Write out the primary messages you tell yourself regularly—the negative self-talk that goes on in your head.

My Inner-Mean Girl Says....

-
-
-

Great! Now it's time to write a counter statement to each of these messages. Anything that speaks TRUTH and genuineness to you.

Example: "Your thighs are so fat," may become "My legs carry me through this world, from point A to point B—and I can squat some mean weight gosh darn it!"

Write them below. Even if you don't 100% believe them yet—this is where change begins to happen.

My New Affirmations:

-
-
-

Looking at that new list, what are your thoughts? Don't believe them yet? It can sometimes be hard to believe the new truth that, "My thighs aren't fat" when you still believe they are, but this is a process and finding new ways to appreciate yourself is part of it.

Here's a **Rule Break Project** to help you see things a little differently.

Write a letter to your younger self.

Give advice to younger you—what you know now that you wish you knew then.

Offer her compassion. Hope. Peace. Encouragement. Warn her about the mean girls or silly boys or insignificant things (which seemed like a big deal at the time) to come. Tell her how you feel about her, how you feel for her. Remind her of her strengths, her values, her worth, her beauty. Anything you want to say to her. Sometimes we are pretty darn hard on ourselves, but if you reflect for a moment on how you would talk to others—especially younger children and girls—you would never say some of the things your inner mean girl says to you!

Practice kindness towards yourself by speaking directly to little you.

Inspiration: Here are some nuggets I passed along to my middle school self in my letter:

1. This too shall pass
2. You are beautiful as you are
3. Go in the direction of your dreams and think bigger
4. The mean girls and popular kids won't always be the top dogs
5. Don't let your BFF pluck your eyebrows
6. You don't have to gloss your lips between every class
7. No one cares if you wore that shirt two weeks ago, they are more concerned with themselves
8. Be kind to everyone—that is true popularity
9. Don't use Sun-In! Your hair turns orange!
10. Leave the cat eye and smoky eye makeup tricks to the makeup artists

11. Don't waste kisses on toads
12. Aim for classy, not trashy
13. Counting calories will only make you go crazy, focus on nour-
    ishing your bod

See what you come up with.

Still not believing in yourself yet?

It's a fact of life that we are our own biggest critic, but that doesn't mean those thoughts are true!

Your Thoughts Are Not Always True

In other words, sometimes you can't trust your own thoughts. The mind is a powerful force to be reckoned with and sometimes, we have thoughts that go through our minds and we don't even question their validity.

For instance:

- *"That's a stupid idea."*
- *"She's so much prettier."*
- *"You suck."*

Any of those ever go through your head? **If so, have you ever questioned whether or not those thoughts are LEGIT?**

Have you ever talked back to your thoughts? Chances are, if you're "stuck in your head," you probably have not.

But imagine the possibilities if you don't believe everything you hear or think, including ideas from yourself or outside sources like Google, BodyBuilding.com, a random blogger or Instagram star, or the news?

After all, when you hear: "The world is flat," do you believe that? There was a time when people did. Our thoughts turn into beliefs that **are not always true.**

Thrive Project:

Put a STOP to the thoughts in your head today. Wear a rubber band on your wrist and when you hear that little voice running through your head, that negative self-talk or negative beliefs, catch it in action and pop that rubber band. The snap will act as a conscious reminder to stop and will help you modify the behavior.

We Are the Stories We Tell Ourselves

Heart (identity) identified? Check.

Inner Mean Girl (the way you cut yourself down) mastered? Check.

You are well on your way to busting through stinkin' thinkin' and reclaiming your own naturally-born healthy, happy, intuitive mindset.

However, we have some more lies to face.

I'm talking about the lies (ahem, stories) you've been telling yourself for far too long—not necessarily about **who you are** (like your inner mean girl), but stories about **who you should be, how you should act, what you should care about, or what you should think.**

We are the stories we tell ourselves, and **the negative messages we whisper to ourselves often become our reality.**

See if any of these common negative stories or thoughts fit with you:

1. I'm so stuck.

2. Ugh, I just want to go back to bed.

3. I can't wait until it's Friday again (living from weekend to weekend).

4. I'm so stressed about _____!

5. I suck.

6. If only I had her stomach, her clothes, her job, her arms, her boyfriend, etc.

7. I'm so fat.

8. I live by my to-do list. First I've got to get this done…then on to that…then next up that… And never feel truly present.

9. I shouldn't do that.

10. I don't want to ruffle any feathers.

11. When I _____ (lose 10 pounds, have more money, buy a house, have a new car, get through this, get this off my plate, etc.), then I'll be happy.

12. I need to be busy and have a stacked social calendar otherwise I'll miss out.

13. Get your act together!

14. You have to do it—there's no other option. *I have no choice or say in the matter.*

15. No one cares about me. I'm so alone.

16. I hate this circumstance, experience, etc.

17. I guess I just have to settle. It will always be this way (my weight, my thoughts, my body, etc.).

18. I should be married (or have kids, be working my dream career, be happy, etc.).

19. Don't let anyone down. Don't let them see you cry.

Aren't you exhausted of all that chatter in your head? If so, it's time for a mindset makeover.

Mindset Makeover: Neural Rewiring

How often do you **think about your own thoughts?** Chances are not much. Your thoughts simply just happen.

Enter: **Mindset ruts**—information that is soft-wired, learned, and thoughts we rarely question. Your beliefs also fall into this category.

Your current brain state **has been taught to think or believe what you've always told it.**

"I'm not good enough." "I'll never change." "This sucks." "I am fat." "I've always struggled with _____." These all come from beliefs you've received from a variety of experiences, outside influences and repetitive thoughts you keep telling yourself.

In other words, you were NOT born to intuitively believe these things or even think negatively.

Toxic thoughts such as these often become protective strategies we use to deal with the moments of defeat, comparison, criticism, insignificance or overwhelm you feel in your health, your recovery, body image, and food.

Pop quiz: As a baby were your thoughts more positive or negative? Did you have judgments? Criticize yourself? Feel down? Have fears?

Short answer: No—at least not in the first six months of life.

Research on the development of **negativity bias** in kids—the idea that people pay more attention to negative things going on around them than positive things—shows that children begin to develop an awareness of **negative thinking** around the time they start crawling and consequently experiencing more fear. More research also claims infants may experience more fear around this time because their mothers start using more prohibitive words like "don't do that" and "no."

By age 4, negative bias becomes second nature, as children themselves begin to use almost double the number of negative words as positive words.

Long story short: **Your negative (non-intuitive) thought patterns, or disconnect from your personal truths in your own head stems from learned (soft-wired) thought patterns.**

The good news?

If your brain can be soft-wired to think *negatively*, it can certainly be re-wired, unlearned or changed to think in new *positive* ways the more actively you choose to re-program it.

Here's an example exercise you can try for yourself to see what I mean.

Reflection & Rule Break Project:
Let's work backwards for a moment with this exercise so you can see how we control our own thoughts:

1. Look in the mirror and tell yourself out loud, "I'm ugly."

2. Repeat this task throughout the day—every time you see yourself in the mirror or pass your reflection, tell yourself that same phrase.

3. At the end of the day, assess how you feel and what you think about yourself.

Chances are...*not so hot,* right?

While this exercise may seem absurd, for many of you, it actually may not be too far-fetched. Some of you already speak to yourself this way without even thinking about it or noticing anymore.

In other words: You are on auto-pilot—conditioned to believe that you are anything BUT beautiful, "good enough," capable, or worthy—no questions asked.

Maybe...

- You hate your nose.

- You know you never get picked first.

- You think you are lazy.

- You're self-conscious about your weight.

- You despise pictures that reveal your profile (side view).

- You don't think you'd get the promotion, so you don't try for it.

- You tell yourself not to speak your mind.

- You look down at your stomach and just wish it was flat, because then you'd be happy.

- You can't stand that your thighs touch.

- You feel awkward in your own skin—too tall, too short, too frumpy, too soft, too lean, too bony, to muscled, etc.

- Or any other negative thought you tell yourself. You name it, you believe it.

How did you come to believe what you do about yourself, your current situation or your worth?

You've told yourself (and others may have told you as well) that's what you should believe.

Remember: So as you think, therefore you become.

When you think in the **negative** (be it about your body, your personality, your value, your job, your social status, your fate, your ability or situation in life, etc.), you live in the negative state of mind.

However, when you think in the positive, talk to yourself in the positive, and imagine yourself as capable and accomplished, you begin to *believe* the positive, speak the positive, do the positive, and make big things happen!

While all the advice to "keep the sunny side up" or "look at the glass as half full" may simply **sound** just warm and fuzzy, science proves otherwise.

For instance:

- An analysis of 32 different studies of self-talk in sports, published in the Perspectives on Psychological Science, indicates that the specific words we use when talking to ourselves also play a role in how well we perform (i.e. **we perform better when we speak to ourselves positively**).

  Phrases like, "Keep your head down," "Let's go now," and "Breathe," helped study subjects focus their attention and trigger the ideal response and action for the tasks at hand.

- Another study with first graders found that after students developed an awareness of the nature of self-talk through a year-long series of lessons (on both positive and negative self-talk) and learned new strategies to change the negative into positive, positive self-talk became **second nature** to the way they thought through things.

- In a 2013 study from the Netherlands, researchers observed women with anorexia walk through doorways in a lab. The women turned their shoulders and squeezed sideways, even when they had plenty of room, indicating the power of the mind: Their internal representation — their brain's perspective on their body — is that their body was much bigger than it is.

- A 2002 study in The American Journal of Psychiatry revealed that patients diagnosed with clinical depression actually recovered from depression after being treated with placebo medicine. In fact, they recovered faster and better than their counterparts who were on actual antidepressants. Again, this shows the power of your mind.

The next time you find yourself speaking in the negative, **catch yourself in the act and flip it to the positive and repeat it:**

- "I've never done that before" to "It's an opportunity to learn something new."
- "It's too complicated" to "I'll tackle it from a different angle."
- "I have always been too _____ (short, fat, quiet, awkward, uncomfortable in my body)" to "I am good enough."

You get the picture.

Take this **neural rewiring exercise a step further** by changing the word "I" to your name or "you," talking directly to yourself:

- "I am so ugly" to "Lauryn, you may feel ugly today, but choose to see the beauty in yourself and what you have to offer the world."
- "I'm always going to struggle with this" to "Lauryn, today is a brand new day of opportunity for the changes you want."
- Or, "I am so stupid!" to "Lauryn, that decision was stupid, but you as a person are not."

Research from the Journal of Personality and Social Psychology suggests that talking to yourself and using the word "I" can actually stress some people out instead of bringing on a feeling of self-love and acceptance.

For example, when superstar basketball player LeBron James talked with the nation about his decision to leave Cleveland for the Miami Heat in 2010, he created distance from himself in his use of language, stating: "I wanted to do what was best for LeBron James," he said, "and what LeBron James was going to do to make him happy."

Becoming an "outsider" to the negative thinking patterns can help you "get out of your own head." That mind of yours is one POWERFUL thing.

16 Powerful Mindset Rules Intuitive People Follow

Tap into your own intuitive mindset superpower with these 16 game-changing "rules" which will help you connect to your natural ability to "be intuitive" in all areas of your life. Redefine your old rules and ways of living with new ones. Starting now.

Rule 1: Maintain a Growth (vs. Fixed) Mindset

A Fixed Mindset is one on auto-pilot, the way of thinking (often negative) that we play on "repeat" without questioning, such as, "I am not good at math." "I'm always going to struggle with my weight." "What if you fail? You are often a failure!"

A Growth Mindset, on the other hand, is one of new opportunity and openness to what could be, what is possible, such as, "Math may not be my strongest skill set, but I love English and words." "I really haven't addressed all the factors that could impact my weight yet." "Most successful people had failures along the way."

Learning to hear your fixed mindset voice can be tricky, especially if you've been stuck in a fix for a long time.

Self-awareness is the process of paying attention to your emotions, needs, physical being, and reactions. By becoming aware of your subtle, ongoing thoughts, emotions, and body, it is possible to detect patterns and take charge of your responses. Start by getting in touch with the presence of your fixed mindset by pausing for a moment to consider YOUR top Fixed Mindset voices that come to mind. Write 'em down.

Realize you have a choice every day: Growth Mindset vs. Fixed Mindset. How you approach challenges, setbacks, criticism, unforeseen circumstances and obstacles is completely up to you.

It's your choice. You can either see them as "things will always be this way" and "change will never happen," or you can face them with a growth mindset, seeing them as opportunities to grow, stretch, expand and conquer!

Similar to our positive spin on our negative comments above, talk back to the fixed mindset voice deliberately with a growth mindset response. Put your dukes up and counter negative thinking with a backlash.

Rule Break Project: Cultivate Intuitive Thinking (the ability to check in with yourself)

Take a moment to get quiet and pay attention to your body, thoughts and emotions.

Are you feeling happy, angry, sad? Are any of your emotions reflected in or caused by the state of your body? Notice your shoulders and neck: can you relax them? As you relax, inhale with a few deep breaths and consider what may be causing any stress, anxiety, tension, or negative thoughts.

Think about your recent interactions and then bring your attention back to the present moment. Think about your toes, and how they feel right now. Move your awareness slowly up your body, starting from your feet. Take a deep breath and resume your day.

Rule 2: Start the Day Off Strong

Intuitive Thinkers wake up ready to take on the day. No, it doesn't mean that they sing with the birds or don't need coffee. But generally, intuitively-connected thinkers live in the moment, starting with the morning, and they happen to the day (as opposed to letting the day happen to them).

You get to choose how your day unfolds, simply based on where you put your energy and thoughts.

Call me crazy, but I love mornings. I love Mondays! I see Mondays (a brand new start to the week), plus mornings (a brand new start to the day) as fresh new opportunities.

It wasn't always this way though. If you'd asked if I liked Mondays or mornings in grad school, I would have told you something completely different. I dreaded the work load, the monotony of class, and long days spent under fluorescent lights. I was not energized by the thought of my day, and most mornings often started off scattered—waking up to my 5 a.m. alarm, running to the gym to squeeze in a slave-driving workout, drinking a quick breakfast smoothie, and trying my best to beat the school bell to get to my desk by 8.

Hurried. Stressed. Exhausted. Until I found a morning routine: New opportunity. And that's exactly what mornings are all about—new opportunities to redefine what it is you want for your life.

You've probably heard the philosophy that "successful people" have a morning routine, things such as:

- Wake up early
- Use an alarm to get a jump on the day
- Workout
- Sip green juice
- Eat a hearty breakfast
- Read something inspirational or motivational
- Stay informed by reading the news
- Drink Bulletproof (butter) coffee
- Get some fresh air
- Stretch
- Pray or meditate
- Acknowledge their gratitudes
- Make to-do lists
- Get their mind right

Author Mark Twain said to get the big work done early, with his famous quote, "Eat a live frog first thing in the morning, and nothing worse will happen to you the rest of the day."

Steve Jobs, of Apple, said he woke up every day and asked himself one thing, "If today were the last day of my life, would I want to do what I am about to do today?"

Every morning when Benjamin Franklin woke up, he asked himself, "What good shall I do today?"

Rule Break Project: Find a morning routine that works for you. Establish your morning routine. Find at least 2 or 3 things you can do to get your day started off strong—and be consistent with them.

Need some inspiration? Here are some of my fave morning "to dos:"

- **3 Things:** I define and list the top 3 things that I would like to "accomplish" or work on for that day. Just 3. I write down my top priorities on a sticky note—and then stick to it.

- **In the Word.** Every morning, I start my "beauty routine" off by reading my devotional, "Jesus Calling." Reading truth reminds me to look up, lean in, pray, and trust.

- **Tune In.** As I cook breakfast, I amp up the latest podcast— typically inspirational—I am in to.

- **Unplug.** For the first 1-2 hours after waking, I have a rule for myself: Don't Check Email or Social Media. Resist. Resist. Resist. The average for most people is within the first 3-7 minutes of waking, we are connected to our phones—checking up on emails, social media newsfeed and the latest news.

- **Get My Greens On.** Every morning includes some form of green goodness—a cold-pressed green juice or sautéed greens with turkey sausage and avocado on top. Popeye power!

- **Iron Belle.** I love strength training in the morning. It helps me clear my head, get the blood flowing in my body, and start my day off strong.

Find your "zen" and begin implementing it this week.

Rule 3: Consume Truth

Have you ever heard, "You are what you eat?" Well you ARE what you put in your mind.

What goes in, comes out (in your self-talk).

What are you "feeding" your mind? In my intuitive mind reset, as I started to fill my mind with truth, I was mind-blown as to what I thought throughout each day.

Thriving Ways to Feed Your Mind

- Read or listen to a mindset growth book
- Encouraging and inspirational music or podcasts
- Starting your day off "right"
- Prayer or Meditation
- Being in a creative flow
- Positive self-affirmations
- Regular dates with good girl friends to just talk
- Positive workshops and seminars
- Asking someone you respect to mentor you and meeting regularly
- Volunteering and community service
- Anything else that you find enlightens your mind!

You play an active role in what goes in—and consequently comes out. The thing is, you probably don't recognize the "negativity" going in, until now. Take inventory of the top "negative" influences in your life.

Reflection & Rule Break Project:

1. What are you filling your mind with that has become "second nature" information or habit?

2. What are the top five topics or questions you've Google searched for the past 24-48 hours?

3. What are the last three things that you read or filled your mind with (blogs, books, articles, etc.) outside of social media?

4. Where do you get your health, food, and fitness information? Are these sources 100% accurate?

5. What outside influences do you fill your mind with on a regular basis?

6. The garbage we put in comes back out (in our thoughts). (And remember: Our thoughts are not always true).

7. How can you de-clutter or minimize them today?

Rule 4: Check-In

One of the most important skills of reawakening your intuition is simply to pause before making a decision, checking in with your gut and your heart, and listening.

When we take the pause or the "check in" out of the equation, we fall into the tendency of leading with our frontal brain lobe (the part of the brain responsible for impulse control, judgement and initiation), rather than including our gut and our heart into the mix.

With this comes second-guessing or "shoulding" ourselves ("I shouldn't eat that," "I should do that"), or the trap of conventional wisdom ("Carbs are bad, so I should eat fewer carbs," "Burn more calories," etc.).

Pausing to check in with your gut before you make a decision, make plans, or let worry-filled thoughts take your mind away has three specific benefits.

The first is that you avoid the risk of going into "auto-pilot" thinking mode—just eating, moving or speaking to yourself, or getting anxious and stressed the way you always have. You're able to check in and perhaps do something differently.

Second, when you pause for a few seconds, you disconnect with your initial judgement(s) of yourself or the decision at hand. Instead of instantly thinking, "How dare you want a piece of chocolate?" and shaming yourself because of it, you instead check in and assess what nourishment that piece of chocolate may actually give you (i.e. It's okay to have chocolate once in awhile).

Lastly, you gain more confidence in your abilities to be able to listen to yourself with the power of a simple pause.

So how do you start your own "power of the pause" reflecting—especially when it doesn't come easily?

Rule Break Project: Breath Journaling

Breath Journaling is journaling style I've created over the years for getting thoughts out on paper. Breath Journaling is an art for capturing your thoughts and reflecting upon them—including your gut and heart into the mix.

Not sure what decision to make? How to process stress or worry? Or what to do today?

Write those thoughts down! All you need is a blank notebook journal or my Thrive Life Project program manual (complete with journal). The methodology is SUPER simple, and helps me keep up with the swarm and randomness of everything going on in that little cabeza (head) of mine.

You have four categories in your Daily Breath Journal:

- Daily To-Dos: Top 3 things I need to do today (At the end of the day, I will feel accomplished if I was able to do these tasks)

- Gratitudes: 3 cool things that happened today (or I am grateful for)

- Prayers: 3 SPECIFIC things I pray for today

- Reflections: 3 cool things I learned today or 3 more gratitudes

- I also have space where I can jot down any extra thoughts or bullets that come to my mind, as well as space to remind me of my BIGGER visions and goals at present.

I call this Breath Journaling because it helps you just breathe…and simplify your mind (or the clutter in your mind) into the power of 3's—3 key focuses in different key areas of your life—and allows you to keep focused on the things that matter most.

If there's one thing I've learned over the years it is this: When I write things down and I keep focused, more gets done, I feel more at peace, and I stay connected to my inner compass.

Note: If writing's not your thing, consider Breath Prayers & Thoughts—moments of intention to release your worries, thoughts and anxieties "up"—pray, ask, reflect, and breathe. Unplug the phone. Turn on inspiring music if it helps and check out for a minute or two. A simple way to remember to do this? Put a reminder on your phone to buzz at a certain time, then stop everything and put the phone aside for a moment.

Rule 5: Make a Mantra

Your mantra is your "fight song"—similar to a mission statement, that reminds you of what you stand for at your core. Your gut intuition.

Most companies and businesses have a mission statement, which is a statement summing up their reason for *why* it is they do what they do and what they *intend* to do—the meaning behind the work of their company in the first place.

Here are some examples:

- Google stands by the mission "To organize the world's information and make it universally accessible and useful."

- Amazon is on a mission "To be Earth's most customer-centric company where people can find and discover anything they want to buy online."

- Nordstrom's' philosophy is "We offer the customer the best possible service, selection, quality and value."

- Whole Foods says, "Our motto—Whole Foods, Whole People, Whole Planet...(We help) support the health, well-being, and healing of both people — customers, Team Members, and business organizations in general — and the planet."

Successful companies and people have a clear mission. Your mantra reminds you of your personal purpose and mission and encouraging to keep your eyes fixed on what you're all about.

Rule Break Project: come up with your own mantra or "Mission Statement"
A phrase, quote, verse, or statement that helps keep you on track and reminds you of why you are working so hard, or what you want for your mindset, your body and your heart.

For instance:

- "I am meant to thrive."
- "Live on purpose."
- "Stop settling."
- "I am worth it."
- "I choose to nourish myself—mind, body and soul with foods, activities, and time spent that brings me to life."
- "I am fearfully and wonderfully made."
- "I have the eyes of the tiger, watch me roar"

- Or a summary statement from your PURPOSE

Your mantra will likely change over time, or you may find you have more than one. That's OK! Just state what comes to mind today. It will help keep you on track and remind you of why you are working so hard, or what you want in the first place. Write the one you come up with on a notecard or piece of paper and stick it somewhere you can see it in front of your face every day (or multiple places).

Remember: So as you think, therefore you become.

Rule 6: Redefine Balance

Balance is one of those concepts we hear about like the "American Dream"—it sounds good in theory, but what does it really mean?

The technical definition of the word "balance" is *"A condition in which different elements are equal or in the correct proportions."*

However, have you ever been completely "equal" in all areas of your life? Picture-perfect equal balance is about as ludicrous as the concepts of an "ideal" body, "perfect" job or "happily-ever-after" relationship—smoke, mirrors or dangling carrots.

That said, balance is still part of a powerful mindset because balance is completely relative to you and when you find that "just right" balance *for you,* life is so much more at peace.

There was a time I felt very unbalanced and my schedule was out of sorts. I hit the gym for upwards of 7 or 8 hours every day and my mind was completely consumed with thoughts about food, calories and exercise. I felt completely starved of the things that I loved to do—writing, connecting with people, athletics, and the ability to be present.

If you were to look at a circle or wheel of my life, and fill in the areas where I spent time, my health, fitness and physique took up about

70% of it, along with most of my thoughts and energy. The other 30%? Whatever brain power and energy I had left went to things like sleep (about 4 hours), school, relationships, daily to-dos and self-development.

So, "redefining balance" during my intuition process became about shifting my priorities and the structure of these self-imposed time con-straints I created for myself and learning to be present. "Redefining balance" also meant redefining my own balance with food, fitness and the expectations of my body—things like:

- Not planning my next meal or day's worth of meals or being so obsessed with eating at the "perfect" time.
- Going out to dinner without calling the restaurant ahead of time to see if they could prep my special meal.
- Traveling without packing my own sweet potatoes, canned tuna, and jump rope to eat "right" and exercise.
- Waking up without dropping straight to the floor to complete 1000 crunches before I allowed myself to eat.
- Learning to be present and at the moment.

What does "balance" mean to you—both in your mindset and in your schedule?

What areas of your life do you feel completely out of whack or bal-ance? Where are you spending more time and energy then you'd like? What is missing in your life?

Redefining Balance encompasses redefining your priorities, your time, your energy expenditures, your thoughts, and your rules.

Rule Break Project: Balance Wheel

Assess your balance on a given day. Complete your own Balance Wheel of Life to get a clear picture of what areas may need a re-shift.

Step 1: Snapshot
Write down a day-in-the-life-of-you snapshot of how you spend your time. From the time you wake up, brush your teeth, commute to work, and beyond, log the hours and time you spend throughout the day - list everything.

Step 2: Circle Up
Using your snapshot for context, make a "balance wheel" for your life. This will include 24 sections to represent the 24 hours in the day. Fill in the approximate amount of time you think you spend in each one of these areas (hours wise).

Things like:

- Work & Education
- Family
- Social, Friends/Significant Other
- Play & Leisure
- Social Media & Online
- Learning & Growth
- Fitness & Health
- Food (Thinking About Food, Prep, Eating or Eating Disorder Habit)
- Spiritual Walk
- Daily Activities (Hygiene, Housework, etc.)
- Commuting & Transportation

Add any other categories that are missing for ways you spend your time that you think are a big part of your days.

Step 3: Reflect
Look at your Balance Wheel—what patterns do you notice? Where are you losing time? What could you be doing differently with your time? Rate each area on a scale of 1-10 with 1 = No energy, time and focus and 10 = A lot of time energy and focus.

Rule 7: Have No Fear

All you ever wanted is on the other side of fear.

"I can't because I'm afraid." This is a lie adults tell themselves that kids have no clue about. We tell ourselves things like:

I can't, because…

- I'll fail.
- They'll laugh at me.
- It's too hard.
- There's no way.

Fear hits you whenever a change or the unknown presents itself—like a change in your lifestyle, flying on an airplane, or having just 5 minutes to prepare for an impromptu public speech. Fear can even hit you when you just *think* about starting something new or different—a new fitness program, a new job, or new way of doing things. And deep down, fear can be overwhelmingly paralyzing.

Unlike your 6-year-old self who never saw any obstacle, defeat, or scary possibility standing in her way, as an adult, you become afraid of not being able to do it at all, or even worse, failing.

Sure kids may be afraid of thunderstorms and monsters under their bed, but kids just don't buy into the lie "I can't do it" or "It's too hard." Quite the opposite: Kids often do the very thing(s) they are afraid to do.

Think about the baby learning to walk. They fall, but they get right back up. Or the kid who gets a "double-dog-dare" to go on the scary "Dragon slide" on the playground. Or the little girl who jumps off the high-dive.

As we grow older and perhaps more seasoned with a few bruises or falls, we talk ourselves off the ledge into this personality trait—fear. The fear of "what could happen." The "I can't" belief because of fear.

Rule Break Project: Do one thing that scares you today.

What have you been letting fear get in the way of?

Think about some things you've WANTED to do like not fear food, try a new breakfast, try a new fitness class, or speak your mind, and also think about what is stopping you.

Then, the clincher: Do *one thing* that scares you today.

No, you don't have to quit your job. It could be something like

- Speaking to a stranger in public
- Reaching out or networking with someone
- Speaking your mind
- Trying a new food
- Trying a new (non-rigid) workout routine or even skipping a workout

Be brave. And just do it.

Rule 8: Social Media Detox

We live in a toxic world—not just our hygiene products and cleaning supplies (chock full of over 85,000 toxic chemicals)—but also our daily media (namely, social media) consumption.

How many times do you check your email and social media—Instagram, Snapchat, Facebook, YouTube, Twitter, LinkedIn—each day? According to Chris Bailey, author of the *Productivity Project*, the number is something like 41-times for e-mail alone in a given day, and an average of 17 social media checks per day, beginning within the first

5 minutes of waking. Other stats report the average U.S. consumer spends a whopping 5 hours a day on their mobile devices. And there's no telling how that number will continue to change with time from date of publication here.

That's 41 times of side-lined attention for e-mails and a social media check for every waking hour, and at least 5 hours out of your 16-17 waking hours devoted to your technology alone.

Sleep plus technology eat up nearly two-thirds of the day! Not factoring in time spent in traffic, daily life management and hygiene tasks—like teeth brushing, showering, meal prepping, eating, commuting and driving, tidying up after ourselves and working.

This is time lost for connecting to our own hearts, minds, and gut.

No wonder we are constantly comparing ourselves and feeling like we "need to get things done." So much time is lost to basic life tasks and phone and media usage, leaving us with very little time leftover for attuning to our hearts and needs—things like creativity, time spent with others, and doing things we love.

Even more soul-sucking for our hearts, minds and gut? According to a survey by Glamour Magazine, more than 60% of us who get onto social media walk away feeling worse about ourselves.

Social media CAN be super toxic if we let it—not only to our productivity in a day, but also for our body image, self-esteem, and going with our gut (instead of what we "should do" or who we "should be"). There's no time like the present to turn over a new leaf (in social media land and beyond!)

Rule Break Project: Social Media Fast

Consider the ways social media impacts how you think and feel about yourself. Go on a social media fast for just one day.

Try it for one full day with no cheating. And then, if you can handle it, go one more day. Notice what comes up for you.

Rule 9: Smash the Scale

Intuitive people don't need numbers to tell them about their body.

You know that scale in your bathroom? Or that once-per-week weight check-in you do for yourself?

It's gotta go. And no. Not "go" as in *hide it under the bed* or *stick it in the closet.*

But GO, as in "smash that scale with a sledge-hammer."

Intuitive people don't look to numbers to define them—what they eat, don't eat, who they are or their worth in the world.

Question: What does that number do for you?

When it's up, what do you feel? Bummed? Like you need to try harder? Like you suck? When it's down, what do you feel? Happy, but more restrictive—if you want to keep it that way, you better continue to work harder? Or happy, like you earned an extra serving of ice-cream? Or scared that you'll lose your edge?

We're damned if we do and damned if we don't.

One more question: How often do you look at other people and see a number written on their forehead? Printed on their shirt? Tattooed on their body? "121." "She's 143." "He's 185."—Rarely.

Most of us don't size others or judge others based on a specific number. Instead we see:

- That cute shirt she's wearing.

- Her awesome haircut.
- A nose ring or tattoo.
- A smile.
- The light in her eyes.

Sure, we may compare our body to hers, but as far as seeing a number dancing over her head? Nope. And you know what? You are not a walking number, either.

No matter what the scale says when you step on and off of it, your name does not change. Nor does your personality. Your skills. Your talents. Your gifts. Your passions. Your purpose. A number does NOT define you. The secret to beginning to believe this?

SMASH THE SCALE.

Rule 10: Master the Permission Monster

Do you remember being a kid in elementary school and asking your teacher if you could use the restroom? "Can I go to the bathroom?" you asked.

"I don't know...*can you?*" Mrs. Hagood smirked, as you stood by her desk, about to pee your pants.

"Puh...puh...puhleassseee...may I use the bathroom?" you said back, ready to sprint to the bathroom regardless of what she responded.

"Yes you *may*," Mrs. Hagood said, and you darted out the door.

From that point on, asking permission to do anything—even to use the restroom—became a battleground for you or at least something that made you think twice, and maybe even brought up feelings of apprehension.

Heck, if something as small as a basic human need (needing to pee gosh darn it) was a big deal to ask for permission, bigger things feel out of the question:

- Asking your boss for a raise after all the hard work and hours you've been putting in lately

- Permitting yourself to take a day or an hour off from the rat race pace you've been keeping lately

- Eating without having to "earn your food" through a purge or workout

- Taking a much-needed break for some R & R: A pedicure, a haircut, a massage, a walk

- Not having to go to the gym at 5:30 a.m. every single day if you went to bed at midnight the night before, or log 3-5 miles in on your run today—because that's what you do *every day*

- Ordering the steak or fish special, instead of the salad

- Scheduling 'you' time into your daily planner—an afternoon workout, a massage, creative space to write or reflect, a meetup group, yoga class you've wanted to try, nothing at all

- Eating the sweet potato, sushi with rice, or piece of fruit instead of fighting so hard to stick to your low carb diet

- Not stepping on the scale every morning to make sure you're 'in check'

- Derailing from your strictly regimented schedule to be spontaneous

- Saying "yes" when you really want to say "no" (Newsflash: you can!)

- Not being so hard on yourself

Need I go on?

Many of you have what I call the "Permission Monster"—the voice in the back of your minds that *needs permission* to take care of yourself, or creates hoops you need to jump through to "earn" your food, your sleep, or time away from work, people-pleasing or perfectionism.

However, in order for any nutrition plan or fitness program to help you get where you want to be, you must acknowledge this fight within you (against yourself) and some of your basic human rights (to nourish yourself, rest, drink plenty of water, move and workout to enliven your energy, do things you love, etc.).

Rule Break Project: Give Yourself Permission

In what areas of your life can you grant yourself permission? Or rather, what areas do you NEED to permit yourself? On this note, how can you eat, rest, move and care for your body out of love, rather than out of fear?

In other words, instead of clinging to food or fitness rules out of the fear of what might happen to your body if you don't follow those rules, how can you shift your mindset in your own self-care to eating, working out, resting well, or more out of love for your new thriving, vibrant, badass self?

Try it.

Rule 11: Create Boundaries

I'll never forget my first middle school boyfriend in the 8th grade, Seth.

Seth was the new kid on the block in my small class of about 100 kids.

A football player with sandy blonde hair and light freckles on his nose and cheeks, all the girls and I thought, "Oh, he's kinda cute," and we were intrigued to know more about him and his story.

It turns out, Seth was my lab partner in 8th grade science and he was rather intrigued by me too.

We made small talk over our frog dissecting experiment. He occasionally let me borrow his pencil when mine broke or I forgot one in my locker. And there was even that one day that he shared his extra stick of gum—just with me.

It didn't take long for Seth to have "feelings" for me, and in return, I told myself I *could* have feelings for him.

So, of course, we became an item.

Seth asked me one Friday afternoon—in a note that his friend Matt passed to me in the hallway—if I would be his girlfriend.

Without two thoughts, I responded "Yes!" (After all, he liked me and I liked being liked!)

Even though I didn't really know Seth much (outside of frog guts and sharpened pencils), I thought he must be sweet *and* I began to envision my first name with his last name and the kids we may have one day together.

Fast forward three weeks later (three weeks too long) and unfortunately, Seth was not the prince charming for me, even though I tried to make myself believe that I liked him.

There was something about Seth that made us not click. I think you call it a "Jock." God bless him, Seth was a classic, stereotypical middle school jock. Not a fan of book learning or conversation aside from football and Mario Kart, and the smell of corn chips and sweat radiated from his armpits when he got nervous, excited or worked out.

We just didn't "connect." However, "love" is blind and I tried for *three* weeks to like him. To *make* myself like him. To the point that I lost my sense of boundaries—the things important to me when it came to "connecting" with the right guy.

- I giggled when he made stupid jokes (which weren't funny).

- I batted my eyes at him—even though I did not feel that way at all.

- I told him I loved watching football—even though it completely bored me out of my mind.

- And I cared about everything he cared about—even Mario Kart and corn chips.

Seth was *not* the one for me and I was not myself with him.

Seth may not have been the one for me, but Seth did teach me (years later) about what I did want in terms of a relationship—someone to connect with, someone who cared to ask me about me too, and someone who I did not need to change my personality or interests for to be liked by him.

Seth also taught me a lesson about having boundaries. Boundaries involve more than rules or limits for dating—they involve knowing (and sticking to) your *inner* values and *who* you are.

Boundaries involve being yourself—not letting people walk over you or change you. They involve having a backbone.

Reflection & Rule Break Project: Boundaries Assessment

In what areas of your life have you let your boundaries go or do you need boundaries in right now?

The things in your life that you let other people's thoughts, opinions or influences shape you, or walk over you, either good or bad?

The beliefs you have about yourself and your worth or how you let other people treat you?

List 'em out. Then…Use your backbone today.

Whatever that means for you. And it doesn't have to be in a spiteful or annoying or mean at all.

It could mean:

- Using your voice and simply speaking up for yourself.
- Just saying "no" (instead of defaulting to your people-pleasing "yes").
- Not saying "sorry" for something you didn't do, or apologizing for someone else's misunderstandings or insecurities.
- Not settling.
- Spending your time wisely—not wasting it.
- Not being a pushover.
- Stopping people pleasing.
- Having (and knowing) your limits.
- Hanging with people who lift you up—don't weigh you down.
- Not conforming yourself to others.

You do you.

Rule 12: Break Busy

We live in a society that feeds off busyness.

Ever caught up with an old friend and asked them what was new? "I am sooooooo busy," they said, glowing.

Or tried to make plans or schedule a meeting? "I am sooo busy," you or the other party said. As a culture, we pride ourselves on our packed schedules.

The MORE we can put in, the better, right? The more productive. The less FOMO (fear of missing out)—at least that's what we tell ourselves.

What does this obsession with busyness do to you? To your inner stress levels? To your ability to just…be?

Answer: Not great things for your mindset.

I'm guilty as charged. I've always been a busy-body, multi-tasker, and multi-to-do-list maker. If my schedule doesn't have something in it, I find a way to fill it. In my eating and body struggles, this tendency was only escalated. As my body and mind were hungry to be "filled"—on multiple levels—the more I sought out my "fill" in a stacked schedule.

The underlying belief? If I wasn't super busy or 'productive,' I wasn't hard-working, important or, worse, a hazard to myself, often acting out more on my tendencies to obsess about food or workout overboard.

The truth is, busyness makes you *less* productive, less in touch with yourself and more stressed overall.

In fact, a study by the University of Michigan showed that switching what you're doing mid-task increases the time it takes you to finish both tasks by 25%.

Microsoft studied this phenomenon in their workers and found it took people an average of 15 minutes to return to their important projects every time they were interrupted by emails, phone calls or other messages. They didn't spend the 15 minutes on the interrupting messages, either; the interruptions led them to stray to other activities, such as surfing the Web for pleasure.

In addition, "being busy" simply stresses us out.

Have you ever been "overbooked" or packed your schedule tightly? What happens? Binge eating, stress eating, flaking out, skimping on sleep or working out, overtraining, spending more money, anxiety, or depression.

Rule Break Project: Slow Down

Evaluate your current schedule. Make a list of some of your personal energy boosters—your favorite 'you time' momenta and slow down activities to help you break the busy cycle, and start implementing them immediately.

Rule 13: Become Type B (Perfection)

"I'm never going to get it!" said my 6-year-old self, crying over my math homework about learning how to tell time with the clock hands. "It's too hard."

Perfectionism runs deep in my blood. For as long as I can remember, if a hair was out of place, my socks were not matching, or I struggled with school or sports, frustration (and sometimes tears) happened. And no matter how many times my mom told me, "It's ok, you will get it," or my teacher affirmed, "You are still learning," my inner perfectionist was stronger.

While perfectionism can seem "good" on the outside (Who doesn't want to be a better person, athlete, student or fashionista?), it will leave you unbalanced because the *ideal* is never achieved.

We all rationally know that "No one is perfect."

Heck, if it takes approximately 10,000 hours to just achieve the minimum of entry-level mastery in any craft, we all have our work cut out for us.

However, it doesn't make false hope go away. The problem is "never feeling good enough," and our constant striving only leaves us with one thing: a feeling of imbalance and lack of peace.

How can you make that inner perfectionist go away? Similar to your inner critic, talk back to it. Do the opposite. Challenge the inner mean girl giving you the ultimatums by facing your fear of imperfection and seeing that it does not negatively impact you.

Rule Break Project: Do something imperfect—on purpose.

Being Type-B actually does a mind and body good!

- Wear an outfit that doesn't match
- Eat breakfast for dinner and dinner for breakfast
- Don't go to the gym today
- Wear your face—makeup free
- Break a food rule
- Wear your hair naturally—just as it is
- Stop saying "I'm sorry" to everyone

Rule 14: Do It Now

"I'll change or do it tomorrow"

This age-old lie is what makes us wake up every day—invigorated to tackle our goals and to-do lists with gusto, only to find ourselves at the day's end, completely exhausted, overwhelmed and saying, "Tomorrow is the day!"

However, tomorrow never comes.

Intuitive people recognize that today is the day! And they move with the rhythms of what is priority in their tasks and to-dos.

Tell yourself: A year from now, you will have wished you had started today.

Next year, what would you tell your current self about the decisions you are trying to make or the changes you keep thinking about?

Heck, even 30 days from now, what will you have wished you did today? What would you right now tell yourself if you could talk to you from 365 days ago?

Change, forming a new habit, or doing something new requires mental effort. But instead of seeing the total overwhelming change (like "gaining or losing 20 pounds," or "cutting out all grains, dairy and sugar" or "taking a balanced approach to fitness," etc.), think about just one thing at a time.

Rule Break Project: Just Do It

Do "the thing" you've been putting off or dragging your feet to do. Make the phone call. Check the bank account. Send the letter. Throw in the laundry. Organize your schedule.

Rule 15: View Life is a Classroom

Why is the sky blue? Are we there yet? Where do babies come from?

Kids are curious—constantly wondering, always learning, and never short on questions. The intuitive mindset never stops growing and is never stagnant.

Unfortunately, somewhere along the way, our mindset about learning changes—like math class.

What was your favorite subject in school? What was your LEAST favorite subject? (Most people have one or two subjects that are their jam—and one or two that are not).

English and writing were definitely my favorites. Math was my nemesis.

I could talk all school day about the themes in *To Kill a Mockingbird* and *The Great Gatsby,* write creative essays and memorize poetry, but come Calculus and Geometry, I watched the clock tick tock, one second at a time. While I passed all of my English classes with straight A's, I struggled way MORE in math—earning B's and sometimes even (gasp!) C's.

Why? My heart wasn't in it and math shut me down.

Learning is way more fun (and an adventure) when we actually enjoy the subject, don't you think? What if we saw life (and learning) the way we did when we were children?

Intuitive-minded people never stop learning and growing

We're never too old to stop learning, and many of the books, seminars, and podcasts I listen to continue to help inspire and influence my own outlook on life. Some of my faves are:

- *How to Win Friends & Influence People* by Dale Carnegie
- The *7 Habits of Highly Effective People* by Stephen Covery
- *The Magic of Big Thinking by* David Schwartz
- *The Slight Edge* by Jeff Olson

What do you like learning about? And what kind of learner are you?

Some of you are hands-on learners—you have to do it for yourself or be there in person.

Others are auditory or visual learners. Think about that in consideration of your Thrive Project today.

Thrive Project: Learn something new today— Anything you want.

A fixed mindset is a stagnant mindset. A growth mindset continues to expand your own horizons outside your fixed bubble (in more ways than one).

- Consider starting a new book—visit the library or download an Audible book.
- Search for a podcast on a topic you're interested in.
- Sign up for a class, seminar, workshop or course.
- Watch YouTube videos about something you've been meaning to figure out or learn, from French braiding your hair to taking the perfect Instagram photo or contouring your makeup.
- Ask an expert or a friend to teach you something new.

Rule 16: No Self-Doubt

The big enchilada: self-doubt.

Enough said. Intuitive-minded people let belief trump doubt.

Even though we will all have bouts of doubt at one time or another, the intuitive mind doesn't rely on conscious reasoning to make decisions. It simply knows.

Back to our little kid self and your "Belle Dress Mindset" that we discussed earlier:

- What did little you think she could be when you grow up?
- What was she capable of?
- Who was she?

No doubt. You didn't then and you must quiet your adult self-doubt to become the intuitive-minded free individual you want to be.

Part 3: Your Intuitive Body

Heart and mind amped up? Now, we're ready to talk about what you *thought* we were going to talk about all along—your relationship with food, fitness, and your body. Remember, to *change* your life or your relationship with any of these things, you must *first* transform your mind and connect with your soul, who you are.

Now for the main event: Starting with a quick gut-check of where you are at today with these things.

Disconnected Body.

"Go with your gut."

It's a message you've likely heard before.

Choosing what college to attend, what shoes to buy, whether or not to stay in a relationship, what to pack for lunch, or deciding what to order at Chili's, our gut certainly faces a lot of pressure to make decisions.

How do you go with your gut, or **listen** to your gut, when it comes to your physical body?

- What do you eat?
- How you choose your food?
- If you drink water, or a Diet Coke?
- Whether you reach for coffee or tea?
- Burger or a salad?
- Whether or not you workout or take a rest day?
- A cookie or piece of fruit?
- How much sleep do you get?

Chances are multiple influences, beliefs and triggers play a role in how you choose your foods, workouts and other self-care habits—outside just **going with your gut.**

Things like turkey burgers...

The Turkey Burger

I didn't feel like a turkey patty. But I *had* to have a turkey patty. It's what I ate every day for breakfast, lunch, and dinner. And I had it carefully calculated into my caloric intake and macros for the day.

I really liked turkey patties. In fact, I was a turkey burger snob.

I'd only eat a specific type of turkey burger—the ones sold at the mom-and-pop body-building gym where I worked out during high school. Come college and graduate school, I special ordered them by the 30- and 60-count bundles, begging my mom to ship them, frozen, from Little Rock to Austin or Nashville—wherever I was living at the time.

Those turkey patties were heavenly pieces of meat. I'd salivate just thinking about them and prided myself on eating "super healthy," because they were a good source of protein to pair alongside my steamed vegetables and Crystal Light meals. They were the only meat I allowed myself to eat.

But this particular day, I didn't feel like eating a turkey patty. I wanted something else. Chicken? Salmon? Shredded pork?

Nope.

How dare I question my beloved turkey patty? I shut myself down. I *had* to have a turkey burger because that's just what I ate. And I knew if I didn't have it, I'd feel worse—guilty, kicking myself, obsessing over whatever I ate instead.

This scenario went down several times over the course of four or five years. Until, one day, I ran out of turkey patties in my freezer, and my next order hadn't made it to my front porch yet.

Forced to choose something else—or not eat at all—I finally had to ask myself: *What do I want? What sounds good?*

I decided I really didn't feel like a turkey patty anyway, and I baked some herb-crusted chicken breasts instead.

As simple as it was, biting into that herb-crusted chicken, alongside my "comfort foods" of my steamed zucchini, broccoli, and beloved Crystal Light, my tastebuds were enlivened. My insides leaped inside—as if to say, "Thank you!"

I was *finally* nourishing my body with something different. Finally giving it some other types of nutrients, flavors and energy.

That day I didn't eat my usual turkey patty, a lightbulb went off:

My body IS speaking…and I haven't been listening.

How about you?

In the remainder of this section, let's talk about the main event in your gut: food, eating and digestion—and raising awareness to your renewed intuitive relationship with it, starting with your beliefs about what you put into your body in the first place.

Your Food Philosophy & Timeline

What is your food philosophy?

This is technically defined as, "Your particular system of philosophical thought about food."

Sort of like your personal values and belief system, but about food.

You know, beliefs or philosophies that govern the choices you make and how you choose your food.

Some of your beliefs may include some of these:

- Food is medicine
- Eat lots of fresh fruits and veggies
- Avoid processed foods
- Avoid _____ (whatever it is you believe you shouldn't have)
- Eating too much makes me gain weight
- I need to earn my food
- Eating is a reward or treat
- Don't waste food—eat everything on your plate
- I don't know where my next meal is coming from, so I better eat up
- I shouldn't eat too much

- If it tastes good, eat it!
- Eating is pleasure
- Eating _____ makes me feel guilty.
- Only eat when you're hungry
- Eat according to a particular schedule, such as six small meals per day
- Food is family—eat in abundance and fellowship with those you love

In other words, What do you think is 'good' to eat? And why do you eat what you eat?

Your food philosophy is personal to you.

For one, it is a reflection of your **identity**—a form of self expression.

Like the teenage girl who finds her identity in pink hair and a nose ring or the young person who decorates themselves with tattoos to show who they are.

Your food philosophy is a **byproduct of your experiences and influences.**

I guarantee that your own food philosophy has been shaped by a variety of influences—from personal experience to magazine articles you've read, mentors you've had, friends or celebrities you admire, advice a personal trainer gave you, something you read on Google, the community you surround yourself with (i.e. 'vegans,' 'paleo people,' Southern culture, etc.).

Think about your current food philosophy and on a piece of paper, in your journal or the space below, jot down your current values about what you eat, food philosophies (what you believe you should eat and why), and your current food rules or food fears. There is no right or wrong answer here.

My Current Food Philosophy:

_____

_____

_____

_____

_____

_____

_____

Ok, now, while you're thinking about food, how about your health philosophy as well?

What is your definition of "being healthy"?

Ask 10 different people and you'll get 10 different answers.

"Being healthy" (to me) is...

- Eating lots of fruits and veggies
- Being balanced
- Not obsessing over food
- Working out
- Losing weight
- Being "pleasantly plump"
- Sticking to a plan
- Peace with food and my body
- Menstruating regularly
- No disease
- Not eating out, smoking or drinking

- Work-life balance
- Having your cake and eating it too
- Sleeping 8 hours each night
- Drinking 8 glasses of water daily

What do you think? Think about these and identify what being healthy means to YOU.

"Being healthy" means:

_____

_____

_____

_____

_____

_____

_____

Now, let's dig a little deeper to understand a little bit more about your philosophies and where they came from. After all, your philosophies have probably changed over the years.

For instance, as a kid, my food and health philosophy was totally one dictated by sugar and additives that lit up my brain—with little regards to how my body felt (except for my tastebuds).

If it tasted good, I'd eat it, and my meals frequently consisted of the foods we know kids love—Goldfish, Cheetos, Lunchables, Pop-tarts and chicken nuggets, with maybe a little broccoli in there if there was cheese sauce on it. I also had an insatiable sweet tooth: Frosted Flakes and Orange Juice, jelly-filled Nutrigrain Bars, Oreos, ice cream. Sweets were a reward and treat, so to attain them, my food philosophy was that I had to earn them or hold them up on a pedestal (by eating my meals, making good grades, winning a soccer game or turning a year older—a birthday celebration).

As a child, the belief system ingrained in me was to finish everything on my plate or in my lunchbox. To earn dessert, I was instructed to "make a happy plate." While this was great parental oversight from a nutrition standpoint, and I have my mom to thank for helping me eat those greens, I became very disconnected with hunger and fullness signals at a young age.

Fast forward to my eating disorder days, and my food and health philosophy completely shifted.

I became obsessed with health—or at least my pseudo-version of it. "Healthy" meant low-cal foods, size 0 and six-pack abs. Food was something I had to earn. My workout intensity determined whether I could have carbs or not. My restriction and denial of calories during the day allowed me to eat dinner with ease at night. And going to bed hungry permitted me to eat a bigger breakfast the next day. I also viewed food as a "toxic" substance. Something that was like poison if I put it in my body.

In my mind, the act of eating and "being healthy" was highly entangled with my weight. Weight gain meant I was "healthy" by treatment standards, but it paralyzed me in fear of being "pleasantly plump" and "robust." Weight loss was a "healthy" pursuit of the eating disorder, but frowned upon by my treatment team. And weight maintenance was a completely gray area of health—I had no idea how to do it.

My ever-changing philosophies of health and weight gain not only stemmed from my skewed views, but also the ones I learned in treatment.

In hospitals and treatment centers, I was often introduced to food as a "means to an end" and something I had to do to get out or earn privileges. Food was meal plans, calories and macronutrients—something I was prescribed, rather than something I chose. Food never felt like a form of "self-care" when Nurse Bertha brought me my hospital tray with chicken nuggets, French Fries, chocolate milk and coleslaw, telling me to "Eat up," or when Nutritionist Lilyan told me during our weekly meeting that her goal was to "Put weight on me so I could have big breasts like her." Food was terrifying, and throughout my eating disorder, I was completely disconnected from "being healthy," "self-care," and "nourishing myself inside and out."

Food and health philosophies can (and do) change over time. How has your food and health philosophy changed over your lifetime?

Your Food Timeline

In this reflection, create your personal food and health belief/philosophy timeline.

You can doodle it, write a narrative or bullet it in the space below, whatever works for you.

Create the timeline of how your food and health story, your philosophy, has evolved and changed over the years to get to where you are now. Reference my timeline story above to see how food shaped me.

You can draw it in this space below, or use a separate sheet of paper to simply draw a line, and mark game-changing moments, years and memories of how your relationship with food has changed over the years.

What do you think?

Your food philosophy has been through the ringer, huh?

When I first completed that exercise, I was shocked at just how big a role food has played throughout my life and influenced not only my beliefs about the food itself, but also my beliefs about myself.

The more I began to understand my belief systems and current relationship with food, the more freedom I began to find with the art and act of listening to my gut and trusting my body.

While this concept may still seem far fetched, try this friendly reminder question (that always helps me snap back to body listening and trust):

What would little-kid me do?

Or what would intuitive m do? (Remember your "Belle Dress")

Time and time again, we will come back to the reminder that kids actually have a lot figured out when it comes to being intuitive.

Think back to being 4 or 5 years old (any time BEFORE self-doubt beliefs about yourself or food lies began to set in).

How did little you decide how much to eat off your lunch tray at lunch? You picked at your bologna sandwich (who liked those anyway?), ate some apple slices, dipped your baby carrots in Ranch dressing, and munched on a few chips.

How did you decide when you told your mom, "I'm hungry?" When you felt hungry.

What did you do when the ice cream melted on your paper plate at your friend's skating rink birthday party? You put your spork down and hit the rink again.

What did you do when your mom cooked dinner for the whole fam? You ate what she served.

Where did you tell your family you wanted to go for your special birthday lunch when they asked you what you wanted? The Purple Cow diner of course! They had the coolest old-fashioned juke box inside and crayons to color on the table paper "table cloth."

You ate based on hunger and fullness. You tried things and developed preferences. You had no clue what calories or diets or ketones or macros were. You enjoyed experiences, socializing and fun atmospheres. You spoke your mind about what you wanted. You didn't make food a big deal. You didn't think about food after you ate it, or fear or obsess over the next meal coming up.

You *simply* ate to satisfaction, nourishment and let your body (and gut) be your guide.

Throughout the remainder of our Intuitive Gut chapters, do a gut check with yourself as needed: What would little (kid) me do?

The Psychology of Eating

Now that you have established your Food & Health Philosophy and Timeline, though more may come up for you later, let's explore how these beliefs, rules, and values sometimes trump your ability to be intuitive—**when your mindset hijacks your body's intuitive cues.**

There are many reasons why we choose to eat what we do and how we treat our body beyond our natural physical cues.

This is called the "Psychology of Eating."

Let's talk about some of the mind games that may inhibit you from eating intuitively, including:

1. Finding Your Identity in Food
2. Disconnected Emotions

3.   Body Image & Self-Esteem
4.   Food Rules & Laws
5.   Stress

Psychology of Eating: Your Identity & Food

Food is self-expression—an identity—and our food choices and food philosophies are often related to both *who we are (our identity)*, as well as who we *want to become.*

In my struggle with anorexia, I identified myself as "struggling with an eating disorder," so in turn who do you think I thought I was? And what do you think my food choices looked like? As I continued to strongly associate myself with "sick Lauryn," I continued to struggle with food, and (subconsciously) aimed to live up this identity—it was comfortable and known. The identity of "the girl with an eating disorder" spurred me on to always *want* and *choose* the most restrictive options—the egg whites, the rice cakes, the 'just getting by' on as little as possible.

Using food as self-expression for the girl I "wanted to become," this also meant choosing the diet, low-calorie, and low-fat options as often as I could. To me, I thought these meant "being thin, pretty and beautiful," something I later discovered was not the case.

Maybe you are an athlete. You identify yourself as an athlete. How do you, the athlete, use and view food? With an athlete mindset on, you may see food as your fuel and eat to perform. You also see the 'bigger vision' of the athlete you want to become—and to shave 1 minute off your mile time, lift heavier or race harder, you use food accordingly. Food is one of your secret weapons for your evolution and athletic endeavors.

Another, say you've "struggled with weight your whole life." With this identity, food is equally a struggle and an often subconscious reflection of this struggle. How does the girl who always hated her weight relate to food? Probably pretty stressed, frustrated and even restrictive with it. Food becomes an expression of her unrest within, and consequently, her stress levels don't help her physical body de-stress, heal, digest, and nourish her body well either. Also, in light of the girl she "wants to be," how do you think her food choices and relationship play out? Diet mentality? A perpetual cycle of restrictive eating then binging? Emotional eating?

Personas aside, other identity markers determine what we eat and how we eat—like our **gender**, **personality**, **stress levels** and **emotions**.

Ever been on a dinner date with a guy you really liked? How did your **gender** influence your eating choices? Research shows that when young males are around women, they tend to eat more. And, in the sorority house at lunchtime, when everyone else was picking salads to eat, what did you choose? You'd look like such a guy if you got the chili dog! Or at a sleepover, when your hair was down with all of your best girl friends, what did you do? Eat popcorn, pizza, and ice cream of course!

Our natural **personality types** influence our identity and food choices. Are you an adrenaline junkie? If so, do you like to live on the edge with your food choices, or prefer stronger, spicier or more ethnic tastes? Or are you cautious and opt for simple, basic food choices, or familiar known foods?

In her book, "Better Than Before," author Gretchen Rubin further describes our unique personality types when it comes to making changes and choices. See if any of those same personality types fit here:

- Are you an **Abstainer**—more impulsive or instantaneous? If so, you may have more difficulty "abstaining" from that plate of cookies or the jar of peanut butter in your cabinet.
- **Moderators** practice the good old 80/20 philosophy of balance (everything in moderation).

- **Questioners** are people who dig into the research, want to know the why's, and make food choices based on research, proof, or validation.

- **Upholders** "just do it"—they take advice and insights from outside sources, or make up their mind to eat a particular way, and just follow through—be it a crash diet they stick out, eating more veggies, or quitting coffee cold turkey.

- **Obligers** *like* to follow the rules—at least on the outside. They may be quick to say, "Yeah. Yeah, I'll do it. It makes perfect sense," but they don't really feel it in their core. It doesn't fit with them. They are people pleasers on the outside, but it's not what they want to do—so they struggle to follow a nutrition plan, or to "make good choices" if it doesn't sit right.

- **Rebels** don't like being told what to do at all—tell em to drink green juice? They drink milkshakes instead.

How do **stress and emotions** influence your food choices? How does food become a "self-expression" or "identity marker" that reflects the tension and stress you feel inside? Are you one who tends to eat more when things seem out of control, or the reverse, eat less or lose your appetite? How is what you eat a reflection of how you feel about yourself or your current circumstances? Does a breakup make you eat more chocolate, or a promotion at work inspire you to celebrate with a special dinner out on the town?

The bottom line: Your identity—the way you see yourself—has a direct influence on your food choices (beyond your physical hunger-fullness cues).

In addition, our food choices (**what and how we eat**) can also shape or influence our identity and the way we stereotype or see ourselves.

For example, say you prescribe to a particular diet philosophy. Pick any one—vegetarian, vegan, paleo, clean eating, etc.

We all have our stereotypes in our minds as to what these people are like:

- Vegetarians are free spirits, crunchy granola heads, bohemian animal activists.

- Vegans do yoga, drink green juices and post lovely pictures on Instagram.

- Paleo people are bacon-eating, Bulletproof coffee swigging, CrossFit cult followers.

- Clean eaters are cooler-toting fitness bunnies, clad in neon workout wear and nosh on egg whites, chicken, protein shakes, broccoli and other tasteless nonsense.

We directly link **what we eat** with **who** people are—including ourselves.

We also connect how we eat with identity as well.

Have you ever known a "**Foodie,**" a person with a particular interest in food, or a gourmet?

Your friend who is always trying a new restaurant or recipe. The gal who throws awesome dinner parties with fancy appetizers and dishes like shrimp pad thai or rack of lamb with au jus, garlic herb potatoes and lemon-infused asparagus? The one who can eat anything—and it goes straight into her hollow leg? She eats ice cream, pizza and salads, freely, and eats using her tastebuds as her guide?

Foodies totally know they are foodies too, and by default, live up to this identity—it fuels their continued love of food.

Have you known an "**Eater**"? Someone who prides his or herself on "being able to eat a whole house," or having "an iron stomach." Eaters love to continually prove that they can eat that much, so they continue to do so.

How about the guy who orders a salad rather than a steak, and chews his food slowly? He's "such a girl."

Or the mom who packs baby carrots and grapes, instead of Cheetos and fruit snacks in her child's lunch box, educating her child on making healthy choices? She's a "health freak."

With so many factors at play, no wonder intuitive eating and food choices are complicated!

Rule Break Project:

Ok. Your turn to think a little bit here:

1. How has food influenced your identity? Examples: "I am a vegan, so I need to live up to that and be authentic about it," or "I am a really healthy eater, and I wrap my identity up in that sometimes."

2. How has your identity shaped how you eat? Examples: "I have always had a sweet tooth, so of course I always reach for sugar" or "I grew up in an Italian family, so we eat—a lot."

3. How would the thriving version of yourself (i.e. your Belle Dress)—and her identity—be shaped (or not) by food choices and the way she eats?

So as you think, therefore you become.

Psychology of Eating: Disconnected Emotions

Like identity, our emotions can influence our food choices beyond our body's natural intuitive cues.

Do you ever:

- Get a little too excited when you see your meal coming towards them at a restaurant?

- Sometimes lose your self-control and can't stop eating something delicious (even though your full stomach tells you otherwise)?

- Wonder what you are going to have for dinner—even though you just ate lunch?

- Try to be "good" all day long—only to reach for whatever is within eye's reach at nighttime?

- Say, "I just get cravings for _____ (popcorn, something sweet, chips and salsa)," or "I TRY to change, and may have a good day...but I always fall back to my old ways?"

Meet: emotional eating.

"Emotional eating" is a term that conjures up images of Ben & Jerry's and a spoon after being broken up with or eating a bag of trail mix because you are bored.

However, "emotional eating" goes far deeper than binging or hiding in closets—and NOT all emotional eating is "bad."

There are two types of emotional eating that hijack our intuition:

1. Mindful Emotional Eating
2. Disconnected Emotional Eating

Mindful emotional eating (MEE) is what happens when you celebrate a birthday with a piece of cake—thoughtfully eating with **happy** emotion. It occurs when you *mindfully or thoughtfully* eat the family lasagna recipe that reminds you of your grandmother who passed with a sense of solemn remembrance. Or mindful emotional eating may even occur during recovery from disordered eating, when you choose to put food rules aside and nourish your body, despite the fear and anxiety you feel.

Disconnected emotional eating (DEE), on the other hand, is the **unhealthy or disconnected** use of food in **response** to emotion, as opposed to a physical need or mindfulness with food.

Signs of Disconnected Emotional Eating include:

- It develops suddenly
- It's above the neck (not a stomach growl)
- It nags (despite fullness)
- It often leads to feelings of guilt and shame
- It's not related to time

DEE is a "heart hunger" and not a stomach hunger, or even social and celebratory hunger, which would be partaking in a festivity, party or another social gathering by tasting or enjoying food—even if you aren't particularly hungry. It is eating to cope, deal, sooth, calm, distract, numb, run, avoid, or fill a void of some sort.

In our effort to band-aid or quiet the emotions we feel, we reach for cookies, pizza, nut butter, French fries, cereal, chips and dip, ice cream, M&M's, and in an instant, an odd sense of mind-numbing euphoria takes the captain's seat (at least for a little while).

DEE doesn't have to involve an all out binge of sugar or junk foods. It can be emotionally eating ice chips, diet soda, turkey burgers, raw veggies or finishing our whole plate (even when we are stuffed).

DEE is an attempt to get something off our mind (sometimes without even realizing). It is an attempt to boost our mood (the serotonin in our brains) with something tangible and pleasurable on our tongue. Anyone who's sought solace in pizza or a pint of ice cream knows that food can be comforting. It is a physical pleasure our bodies get through artificial ingredients, additives, sugar, fats, the act of chewing or eating, and other 'comfort foods'—a biological response our body has as well, triggering a psychological response to eat more of it.

And DEE is *not just in your head* (or a matter of "just making up your mind not to do it"). Research points to the magnetic pulls of food and the impact food has on our mood.

In one study, researchers at UCLA evaluated the brains of women with and without bulimia. They showed the women pictures of a chocolate milkshake or water and gave them tastes of both, all the while examining images of their brain using an MRI. Women with bulimia nervosa who reported experiencing negative emotion just before the experiment exhibited **greater neural activation in their brains** in anticipation of the milkshake. In short, when a bulimic woman is sad, for example, her brain reacts strongly to the thought of drinking a milkshake.

A study in the *Journal of Clinical Investigation* found the foods we eat can have a psychological impact. It involved researchers injecting one of two "meals" into the stomachs of 12 healthy, normal-weight volunteers: a solution of saturated fatty acids, or a saline control solution. (Note: The researchers used a fat-based solution since comfort foods are often fatty, and they were familiar with the brain's response to the solution from former research). After the feeding, the researchers induced feelings of sadness in the volunteers by playing sad classical music and showing them images of faces with sad expressions.

Mood surveys administered throughout the experiment revealed that the **participants found the sad music considerably more depressing after receiving the saline solution than after the fat solution**. MRI brain scans supported that compared to the saline solution, the fatty solution appeared to dampen activity in parts of the brain involved in sadness and that responded to the gloomy music.

Translation:

1. Emotional eating can become a habit—but is rooted in some sort of emotional trigger.
2. Emotional eating is not just in your head. Food can have a physical impact on your body—disconnecting your brain from your body.

DEE, or "heart hunger" is the type of eating generally experienced in a disordered or funky relationship with food.

Psychology of Eating: Stress

Another emotional eating trigger is stress, which is yet another mind game when it comes to your ability to **trust** your body.

There are two types of stress that can take away from your natural intuition:

1. **Physical Stress** (i.e. restrictive diets, binge-purge, processed foods, medications, overtraining)
2. **Mental Stress** (i.e. hating on your body, worry about food, food rules)

Most of the times, when I talk to a client about "stress," or ask them if they are stressed, they instantly think about mental stress alone.

"Well, no I am not anxious." Or, "No, I manage my time really well."

Stress also involves how we feel about and treat our body.

Do any of these sound familiar?

- Constantly burning a candle at both ends?
- Never enough time in the day?
- Take prescription medications or antibiotics for longer than seven days?
- Eat processed or packaged foods frequently?
- Addicted to stevia or artificial sweeteners?
- Restrict your dietary fats or carbs?
- Run 5 or 6 miles every day?
- Don't feel complete unless you've beat your body up in the gym?
- Skip meals?

- Frequently experience gas or bloating?

Hello, stress!

Since stress is the number one driver of disease and imbalance, when we are stressed over food, or stress our bodies out using food (by restricting food, food rules, binging), it's no wonder "listening to your gut" is complicated.

Like most things, there is not just a mental or emotional science to this, but also a physical science as well.

I call this the "Brain-Gut connection"—a stressed out body or gut, stresses out and influences your brain, mindset, and intuition as well. The "Brain-Gut connection" is essentially what it sounds like: **Your gut and brain are directly linked.**

Have you ever gotten butterflies in your stomach before giving a speech or singing in your 5th grade talent show? Brain-gut connection.

Ever not felt hungry right after a hard workout? Brain-gut connection. **Fun Fact:** working out actually raises cortisol—your stress hormone—and suppresses hunger cues.

Your vagus nerve, which is the nerve responsible for a lot of your thinking and brain function, is connected from the top of your stomach, all the way up to your brain.

Your gut uses the vagus nerve like a "walkie talkie"—the gut talks to it to tell your brain how you feel ("those gut feelings" or "butterflies in your stomach"). Conversely, your brain talks to your gut to also tell it how you feel (public speaking fears anyone?).

Couple this with the fact that your GI tract is lined with more than a hundred million nerve cells, and it makes sense: **the inner workings** of your digestive system don't just help you digest food, but also guide your emotions.

So, when your gut health is unhealthy or imbalanced, so is your brain and intuition.

The Bottom Line: The health of your gut "micro-biome" is an essential ingredient in your recovery from *non-intuitive* eating, (as well as stress management). If you want to manage stress, and *re-awaken your natural intuition*, start with healing your gut and balancing your bod.

Psychology of Eating: Body Image & Self-Esteem

Remember this? "When I lose 10 pounds…"

In our efforts to reach an ideal body or aesthetic goal, we often silence our intuitive eating skills. We turn off our ability to "listen to our body" in the name of whatever rules or regulations we need to follow.

We eat and drink nothing but juice for seven days in a row. We swear off carbs and feel guilty if the mere thought of a sweet potato crosses our mind. We obsess over hitting macros or staying under our calorie limit for the day, calculating it all on My Fitness Pal.

What's the "craziest" diet, food rule or body hack you've tried—in the name of improving your body or body image?

The problem? 99% of diets fail. They don't last. And you **stress your body and mind out thinking about food and your body.**

After the seven days, 30 days, or three months are up, we are so over it, and even if we have reached our "ideal" body, the majority of quick fix diets are **not sustainable.** We never once thought about listening to our body in the first place all that time.

So what happens?

Our body cues for food turn back up. After being suppressed for those seven days, 30 days or three months, our desires and thoughts (or obsessions) about food are louder than before, as our fight and flight survival mechanisms come out to play.

The human body is wired for survival and desires optimal *balance* or *homeostasis* above all. Most diets are not balanced, and, to a degree, you feel deprived (either physically or psychologically). When we deprive our bodies of the full nourishment and needs it has, our bodies and minds are starved.

In response, to let us know, "I need food"—our brains turn to *thinking, longing, obsessing, craving and even dreaming about food.*

On of the most powerful illustrations of the effects of restrictive dieting and weight loss on behavior is an experimental study conducted over 50 years ago at the University of Minnesota. The observational study involved 36 young, healthy, psychologically "normal" men while restricting their caloric intake for six months.

More than 100 men volunteered for the study as an alternative to military service, and the 36 selected had the highest levels of physical and psychological health, as well as a highest commitment to the objectives of the experiment.

What makes the starvation study or "semi-starvation study," as it is now commonly known, important is that many of the experiences observed in the volunteers are the same as those experienced by individuals with eating disorders.

During the first three months, the participants ate normally while their behavior, personality, and eating patterns were studied in detail. During the next six months, the men were restricted to about half of their former food intake and lost, on average, approximately 25% of their original weight.

Although this was described as a "semi-starvation study," it is important to note that cutting the men's rations to half of their former intake was identical to the caloric deficit comprising "conservative" treatments for obesity.

The six months of weight loss and "semi-starvation" were then followed by three months of rehabilitation, during which the men were gradually re-fed. And an additional subgroup was followed for almost nine months after the re-feeding began.

In the end, results were reported for 32 men (Four men withdrew either during or at the end of the semi-starvation phase): Although the individual responses to weight loss varied considerably, all men experienced dramatic physical, psychological, and social changes. And in most cases, these changes persisted during the rehabilitation or re-nourishment phase.

The most striking change that occurred in the participants was a dramatic increase in preoccupation with food. Men found **concentration on their usual activities increasingly difficult, because they became plagued by incessant thoughts of food and eating.**

In fact, during the semi-starvation phase, food became the main topic of conversation, reading, and daydreams. **Evaluation rating scales revealed that the men experienced an increase in thinking about food, as well as corresponding declines in interest in sex and activity during semi-starvation.**

Other research observations included:

- As the starvation progressed, the number of men **who played with their food** increased.
- During the restrictive dieting phase of the experiment, all of the volunteers reported **increased hunger** that led to **episodes of binge eating.**

- They ate and prepared foods which, under normal conditions, would be **weird and distasteful dishes.**

- Those who ate in the common dining room often **snuck food** back to their rooms to consume on their beds in a long-drawn-out ritual.

- **Cookbooks, menus, and cooking became intensely interesting** to many of the men who previously had no interest in nutrition or food.

- The participants often reported that they **experienced pleasure from simply watching other people eat or from just smelling food.**

- They used stimulants and gum to curb hunger. **The consumption of coffee and tea increased so dramatically that the men had to be limited to nine cups per day**; similarly, gum chewing became excessive and had to be limited.

- The volunteers reported impaired concentration, alertness, comprehension, and judgment during semi-starvation, however, formal intellectual testing revealed **no signs of diminished intellectual abilities.**

- As the six months of semi-starvation progressed, the volunteers **exhibited many physical changes**, including: gastrointestinal discomfort, decreased need for sleep, dizziness, depression, headaches, hypersensitivity to noise and light, poor motor control, edema (an excess of fluid causing swelling), hair loss, decreased tolerance for cold temperatures, visual disturbances (i.e., inability to focus, eye aches, "spots" in the visual fields), auditory disturbances (i.e., ringing noise in the ears), and paresthesias (abnormal tingling or prickling sensations, especially in the hands or feet).

- Even after 12 weeks of re-feeding, the **men frequently complained of increased hunger immediately following a large meal.**

What does this mean for you?!

Whether you've had an eating disorder or not, if you've ever been on a strict diet, tried "really really" hard to lose weight, get caught up in weighing yourself, calorie counting and perfect eating, there are physiological and psychological reasons why you can't stop thinking or obsessing about food.

Your body is stressed and not getting what it needs.

The bottom line: When we base our food choices more on our outer appearance, program checklists and food rules, stress (over food and our body) hijack our intuition.

What Kind of Hungry Are You?

There are a total of **7 different types of hunger**—often confusing your ability to be intuitive if you are relying on stomach hunger alone.

These include:

- **Stomach** Hunger: Empty feeling, growl in your stomach
- **Cellular** Hunger: Physical need and deficiencies of body for nourishment
- **Taste** Hunger: Tasting food and getting hungry
- **Sight** Hunger: Seeing food and getting hungry
- **Smell** Hunger: Smelling food and getting hungry
- **Head** Hunger: Thinking about food
- **Heart** Hunger: Emotional hunger

Here's a brief overview:

7 Different Types of Hunger: Which One Are You Actually Feeling?

1. **Stomach Hunger:** The physical hunger your body feels when it's tank is empty. A growling or empty stomach is often a sign. You can even train yourself to feel stomach hunger. You may have experienced this if you've ever been on a schedule, such as eating breakfast, lunch and dinner at approximately the same times every day. To determine your physical level of hunger, before your meals, try to **assess your hunger on a scale from 1-10 before a meal (1=famished, 10=stuffed).** Halfway through, check in again and do the same.

   Food for Thought: Awareness about what you've eaten and drunk that day can play a big role in determining your "physical hunger." The same part of your brain that tells your body it's hungry (your hypothalamus) also tells your body when it is thirsty. Often, folks confuse hunger with thirst if they have not properly been hydrating throughout the day. Remember: you need at least half your bodyweight in ounces of water per day.

2. **Cellular Hunger:** Your body NEEDS nutrients—and needs them now. This is the type of hunger where you may have felt an *inner craving* for something, like red meat or other protein source (iron), oranges or fresh squeezed orange juice (Vitamin C), buttery spread or creamy almond butter (fatty acids), pickles (sodium), leafy greens and fresh vegetables (more vitamins and minerals—especially after some meals of junk or sugar), or chocolate (magnesium). Similar to checking in with your hunger in point 1, **check in and assess your body's needs— especially when you think it may be hunger. What are you truly hungry for?**

Food for Thought: Interestingly, many people try to satisfy their true cravings in as many ways as possible other than what they are ACTUALLY craving.

Take a "dieter" on a low-carb approach...their brain and body may be craving carbs (especially if they workout or lead an active lifestyle), but in their attempt to "stick to the protocol", they try to satisfy that cellular hunger (for glucose, B-vitamins, etc.) through more protein only to still feel hungry (cellular hunger). Are you truly listening?

3. **Taste (Mouth) Hunger:** Salivating for a bite of chocolate cake? Creamy ice cream? Cheesy pizza? A hearty bowl of veggies or refreshing salad? Whatever we think of as tasty, appealing and satiating food is often conditioned—socially, habitually or influenced by our upbringing (i.e. mom's home cooking or "Southern food," Tex-Mex, ethnic food, etc.). For some, this means fast food or sugar. For others, veggies, crisp refreshing salads or hearty meat and potatoes make their mouths water. Mouth hunger has a HUGE brain-body connection. Are you really hungry—or are your tastebuds?

4. **Sight (Eye) Hunger:** Similar to those tantalized taste buds, eye hunger is the "in sight, in mind" kind of hungry wherein you *crave it* and hunger for it as soon as you see it. To satisfy your eye hunger, consider actually focusing on your food—and the presentation of it—at your meals. Instead of mindlessly watching TV or ignoring the food before you, engage it visually. Take time to make a nice plate of your presentable meal, rather than quickly stuffing your face with food in your lap while driving or eating straight from the container.

5. **Smell (Nose) Hunger:** Taste is very closely linked to the smell of food. Who hasn't smelled chocolate chip cookies baking in the oven and not thought of hunger or eating? Or smelled warm stew or chicken soup on the stovetop and wanted a

hearty bowl then and there? Maybe you smelled fresh cilantro and thought, "*Hmm…Mexican food sounds good.*"

The process of eating, digestion, and satisfaction through food begins before the food even touches your tongue. It begins with the thought, and often those thoughts are spurred on by nose hunger. Are you hungry because of what you just caught a whiff of? Do you satisfy your hunger with food that is sensory-fulfilling and pleasing? Enjoy the smells of your food for nose-hunger satisfaction.

6. **Head (Mind) Hunger:** Ever find your mind easily wandering? One minute you are thinking about checking off your morning to-do list (dry cleaners, bank, text Sarah, e-mail Rick, etc.), and the next you are thinking about the spat you got into with your significant other last night and then what you want to "be when you grow up" (your next career move).

   The mind is constantly shifting and changing thoughts and directions (we have approximately 50,000 to 70,000 thoughts every day), hunger and thoughts about food included.

   When our mind is anxious or worried, food can bring a sense of tangible steadiness and 'peace' for a time. When our mind is stressed, food can bring a sense of peace and calm through pleasant tastes, and chemicals that light up our brains (like serotonin—the feel-good brain chemical). When our mind is adamant about adhering to diet rules and protocols we've been told, then we stick to those rules and regimes with no second thought about anything different. *Mindfulness* about how those (thoughts, beliefs, stressors and concerns) are affecting your hunger can bring new awareness to "listening to your body."

7. **Heart Hunger:** The mac-daddy of them all. Heart hunger is the most connected to your **emotions**—how you feel in your soul.

For instance, you might consider certain foods "comfort foods," because you ate them as a child, or because you've associated it in our mind as a treat for when you're feeling down. Other foods may be "trigger foods" because you got sick eating it before, or every time you eat that one type of food, you tend to binge or overindulge.

Often, heart hunger boils down to a desire to be loved or cared for, or to fill a hole or void, which ultimately cannot be satisfied through eating.

Feeling "not good enough," "bad about yourself," "frustrated with being stuck," "unloved," "down on yourself," and other negative feelings are all circumstances when heart hunger may take over your body's hunger cues.

To satisfy your heart hunger, you need to find the void your heart is craving. As you stop to think about it, try noticing the emotions coming up around your need to snack or eat. What are you really wanting?

So what can you do to make Disconnected Emotional Eating "go away?"

Stick with me. We will talk all about how to *"Redefine"* your relationship with food (and your emotions) later in this book, as well as continue to raise awareness to some new insights for regaining your intuitive eating skills, but here are some initial tactics to get started:

1. **Check-In.** Ask yourself: What am I reaching for? What am I trying to fill? Is it:
   o Meaning and Purpose
   o Autonomy (independence)
   o Safety
   o Empathy
   o Sustenance (food, nourishment for body, mind and spirit)

- ○ Creativity
- ○ Love
- ○ Community
- ○ Rest/Relax/Play

Until you can answer this question, your habits are going to continue. Connect with a counselor, mentor or friend about your epiphany to gain support and accountability in moving forward.

2. **What Type of Hungry Are You?** When "hunger" strikes, check in with yourself to assess what type of hunger you're feeling. Reread the seven types of hunger and ask yourself if any fit with how you currently feel.
   a. Am I seeing food, which made me hungry?
   b. Is my stomach growling?

3. **Eat balanced meals throughout the day.** Set your body (and brain) up for success to not subconsciously need to reach for "whatever." Incorporate protein, carbs, veggies, and healthy fats into every meal. This helps with balance.

Food Rules & Myths (You Believe)

Sometimes we let the myths we believe about food overtake our intuition with food.

From the time **I was 10 years-old to 24, I was always on some sort of diet—bound by rules and perfection.** Vegetarian. Low-fat. Paleo. Low-calorie. 'Clean-eating.' All-fruit cleanse. I felt extremely guilty if I ever broke my rules, until I learned that many of the food rules I followed were actually not true.

Rules were made to be broken. Here are 16 common food rules, or myths, you may have believed (and truths to set you free).

1. Don't Eat After 8 P.M.
2. Eat Six Small Meals Every Day
3. Egg Yolks, Red Meat & Butter Cause Heart Disease
4. Take a Calcium Supplement & Eat Low-Fat Dairy for Strong Bones
5. Eat Lots of Whole Grains
6. Go Gluten Free
7. Soy is a Great Protein Source
8. Drink Coffee to Boost Metabolism
9. Replace Sugar with Artificial Sweeteners
10. Fruit Makes you Fat
11. If It's Organic, It's Good For You
12. A Detox or Cleanse is a Great Way to Rewire the Body
13. Save Up for a Cheat Meal
14. Eat 1200 Calories Every Day
15. I Must Workout to Earn My Food
16. Cookies Make You Gain Weight

Myth 1: Don't Eat After 8 P.M.

Truth: Timing is not as important as you may think.

Your body is not bound to the same 24-hour clock you and I are (ex. "Lunch is at noon"). Instead, it views food as fuel, and within a 24-hour cycle, as long as it is getting fed and nourished regularly and adequately, it does not care about the timing or even the names of the meals you have. For instance: it sees "breakfast" as "Meal 1", lunch as "Meal 2" and late night snack as a "little bit of extra nourishment"—especially if you are genuinely hungry for a little something.

The only reason you may want to consider timing is digestion. Lying down right after eating can slow the north-to-south process of digestion. However, if you find you are still hungry before bed, I often recommend sleeping with your head propped up at an angle and taking digestive support—like digestive enzymes—to support proper digestion.

Myth 2: Eat Six Small Meals Every Day

Truth: Allowing 4 to 6 hours between meals is NORMAL.

It gives our bodies time to digest what we've eaten and then lets our gut rest for a while. You're not a cow and you don't need to graze all day.

Contrary to popular belief, eating six times per day doesn't "rev" your metabolism or any of the other claims you hear. What does it do? Puts a constant demand and stress on your digestive system and blood sugar balance. The process of digestion takes anywhere from 6-8 hours just to work through your small intestine (the place where the majority of our digestion happens).

When we are constantly starting and stopping eating, starting and stopping eating, we send our digestion and blood sugar levels on ups and downs, leading to things like headaches, shakiness, anger, obsessing over food, and energy dips. If you find yourself hungry 2-3 hours after your meals, try eating a little more at meal time (Especially healthy fats. Are you getting enough?).

Note: Snacking is not a "bad" thing and can ALSO be part of an intuitive eating. The main point is to focus first and foremost on eating enough balance at meal times for optimal digestion and healthy blood sugar levels, then *listen* to your body between meals.

Myth 3: Egg Yolks, Red Meat & Butter Cause Heart Disease

Truth: Conventional advice from most nutrition books and news reports tell us that fatty foods can be good.

Contrary to popular belief, fatty foods like red meat, whole eggs and butter do a body good. These foods:

• Build stronger bones

- Improve liver health (Your liver rids your body of wastes and toxins)
- Decrease cardiovascular risk factors (healthy fatty acids and amino acids from sustainably raised meats prevent inflammation)
- Boost healthy brain function (Your brain is made of fat and needs saturated fats as well as amino acids to feed it)
- Strengthen the immune system (Fat strengthens our cells to defend against disease)
- Promote proper nerve function and signaling
- Make food taste GREAT!

"But what about cholesterol?" you ask. True, saturated fats are associated with having cholesterol, but, guess what? The cells in your body are made of cholesterol, and to be made stronger (more supple, less body fat, less disease)—they *need* some cholesterol to support their cell wall structure. Moreover, research shows that the cholesterol scare is NOT something to be fearful of nowadays. 70% of heart-attack patients' cholesterol levels did not indicate "cardiac risk" (i.e. they don't have high cholesterol, and cholesterol had nothing to do with their heart attack).

The real culprits of heart disease, poor health and stroke risks are stress, poor gut health, trans-fats, sugar, additives and other processed foods.

In a study on the connection between dietary intake and heart disease, researchers found that, out of the 700,000 deaths observed from heart disease, only about one-third of those deaths (250,000) were associated with excess consumption of saturated fats. However, *twice* that amount (537,200 deaths) were related to consumption of large amounts of trans fats, found in foods like packaged cereals, bars, chips, processed diet foods and frozen foods with additives, conventional deli meats, baked goods, fast food, takeout and foods cooked in vegetable oils at restaurants.

The moral of the story? Saturated fat (grass-fed red meat, pastured egg yolks, grass-fed butter and dairy, ghee, tallow, lard, duck fat, coconut oil and coconut butter) does a body good.

Myth 4: Take a Calcium Supplement & Eat Low-Fat Dairy for "Strong Bones"

Truth: Not all dairy products or supplements are created equal.

1. **Fat-free sources are processed foods.** When we eat dairy *without* healthy, natural fats (such as grass-fed milk, full-fat organic plain yogurt, hard cheese), our bodies don't digest the minerals and nutrients in the first place (fat is necessary for absorption) and are also more prone to inflammation from processed foods.

2. **Calcium supplements are not always necessary.** Most people are actually not deficient in calcium in the first place. Instead, they lack other minerals which help us absorb and digest calcium, including, phosphorus, magnesium, Vitamin D and Hydrochloric acid. Your body cannot utilize isolated calcium unless calcium is paired with these cofactors.

3. **Calcium supplements are connected to increased risk for heart disease.** A study of 24,000 people found those taking calcium supplements had a 139% greater risk of heart attacks during the 11-year study (And calcium-rich foods did not increase the risk).

4. **Calcium isn't just found in dairy.** Calcium-rich foods can be a healthy way to consume enough calcium for your body without overdoing it. However, dairy is not the only source. Other great sources of calcium include greens, broccoli, full-fat kefir, sardines, almonds, sesame seeds, okra, figs, oranges, dried apricots, and canned salmon.

Myth 5: Eat Lots of Whole Grains

Truth: Unfortunately, most grains found in grocery stores today are highly processed, difficult to digest, and irritate the gut.

Since the inception of the food guide pyramid in 1992, the USDA has asserted that Americans should consume 6-11 servings of whole grains per day, more servings than any other food group in the pyramid. Whole grains include whole wheat bread, brown rice, sprouted grains, bagels, oats, tortillas, pasta, and more.

Many believe 'whole grains' must be good for us, right? Not quite.

Grains are comprised of a hard outer layer (bran) that contains two "anti-nutrients" called Phytic Acid and Lectins. These "anti-nutrients" are meant to "protect" the grain from predators and weather in the wild. When consumed by humans though (even though we cook them), many of this Phytic Acid and Lectins bind to nutrients inner food and inhibit the absorption of calcium, magnesium, iron, copper and zinc. When consumed frequently, our digestive system also struggles to break these grains down properly, viewing these anti-nutrients more like "steel bullets" in our gut (similar to trying to eat a whole potato without fully roasting it; or a dinner-plate full of raw broccoli and Brussels sprouts alone for supper—difficult to digest).

"So I *shouldn't* eat grains?" Not so fast. Within the context of 80/20 balance and intuitive eating, there is *no such thing* as good or bad foods, and there can certainly be a time and place for grains. Try soaked and sprouted grains like rice, quinoa, and steel-cut oats (i.e. soaking your grains in water overnight before cooking to helps release anti-nutrients from the shell).

Myth 6: Go Gluten Free

Truth: Check in and experiment if gluten works for your body

Deciding if certain foods fall into your personal dietary intake really comes down to getting in check with your body (both digestive symptoms and other "gut imbalances"):

- Do you break out when you eat it?
- Experience gas and bloating?
- Allergies flare up?
- Constipation happens?
- Bloating and gas?
- Joint pains or stiff joints are your norms?
- Do you get frequent yeast infections?
- Do you have a weaker immune system?
- Don't understand why you're always so anxious or worried?
- Have hormonal imbalances or crazy PMS?
- An autoimmune condition?
- Frequent headaches?
- Get stuffy or sinus congestion easily?

If so, chances are something in your diet is impacting you. It COULD be gluten...or it could also be other cross-contaminating foods with gluten (like instant coffee, corn, soy, eggs, tapioca, and other grains). Gluten is not the only "enemy."

The wheat, gluten and grains we eat today are completely different than the wheat, gluten and grains of the days of old.

Before 1910, **70% of all bread eaten in the U.S. was baked at home, stone ground and fermented**. Come 1961, practically 0 bread was baked at home when the processed food industry began using more high-speed mixers, cheaper wheat, chemicals, solid vegetable fat, commercial yeast and water, in the majority of their products. The result? Many gluten AND gluten-free products contain additives, ingredients and hydrogenated oils beyond gluten that our bodies struggle to digest.

Should YOU go gluten free? The best way to determine if gluten is affecting you is to ask: How does this food make me feel?

Food intolerance tests (such as Cyrex Labs) can also be beneficial for assessing your gluten tolerance, as can an elimination period, which means cutting out gluten-containing foods, then re-introducing one at a time, after at least seven days. Note how you feel, both physically and mentally.

If you don't have gluten sensitivity, then your body won't respond differently. Just like if you stopped eating apples for a year or two—with no sensitivity issues—then decided to eat an apple again. Your body would simply say, "Cool. Thanks for this delicious apple!"

If you *do have a gluten sensitivity, you will see or feel a difference*. Similar to a dirty windshield, if your windshield is full of dirt and there is a little speck of dirt on it, you are not going to notice it, but if you have a clean windshield and a speck of dirt gets on there, that speck of dirt becomes very noticeable.

Fun fact: 1 in 2 people with celiac disease—severe gluten allergy—don't have digestive symptoms. Instead, they experience symptoms like brain fog, fatigue, or a suppressed immune system.

Let your body speak for itself and listen.

Myth 7: Soy is a Great Protein Source

Truth: Although soy is a legume and contains all the essential amino acids, these proteins are not always digested or used by the body.

The issues with all legumes are, by nature, they are also designed to be protected in the wild from predators and weather. Beans contain a special shell casing made up of phytates and lectins (similar to whole grains) to help them do just that—not be eaten by other animals or destroyed by vast storms. This is great for the beans and legumes, but not great for our human guts.

So, even though it *is* a good thing that soybeans are a "real food," their **in-digestibility** makes them questionable (and that 9-grams of protein in your Kashi cereal insignificant). Additionally, many of the processed, heated, and packaged versions of soy are just like any other processed food—not ideal, such as tofurkey, seitan veggie bacon, soybean oil or protein in your granola bar or 'protein' chips, Kashi Crunch cereal, and more are processed versions of soy with **zero** noted health benefits).

The best options?

Real food: real, whole, soy sources (i.e. not processed, fermented, additive-filled, and as close to the real deal as possible), like Tempeh, natto, fermented tofu, miso—all in real, whole-sourced, fermented forms.

Myth 8: Drink Coffee to Boost Metabolism

Truth: When consumed in abundance, coffee decreases metabolism.

Approximately 85% of Americans drink coffee—and not just one cup! On average, they drink three cups per day, often with added sugar.

Like most things in life, coffee is not inherently bad, but since coffee is a natural stimulant (i.e. stressor), high amounts of coffee can promote blood-sugar imbalances, hormonal imbalances, digestive dysfunction and metabolism mayhem.

It all comes down to blood sugar and cortisol (stress hormones). Coffee, even decaf, directly impacts these two things by elevating them. When you spike your blood sugar and stress hormones day in and day out with *lots* of coffee, your hormonal balance and metabolism take a hit.

As cortisol goes up, the blood sugar and hormone balance get out of whack, provoking symptoms like: fatigue; frequent cravings for sugary snacks and caffeine; stubborn weight gain; digestive disturbances; poor sleep; afternoon crashes; feeling "wired and tired" at night; frequent urination or thirst.

So what do you do to suppress symptoms? You reach for more coffee, sugar, exercise, or another stimulant to help you feel "balanced"—for the short term. It's a perpetual cycle.

Also, did you know that coffee (particularly instant coffee) is the most cross-contaminating food with gluten (or "gliadin")? If you are sensitive to gluten, consuming poor-quality coffee regularly can also wreak havoc on your body and metabolism. One cup of quality, fresh, organic whole roasted beans is the way to go if you do drink coffee.

Myth 9: Replace Sugar with Artificial Sweeteners

Truth: Your body sees artificial sweeteners like it does sugar.

Artificial sweeteners a linked to a host of side-effects just as "bad" as high-sugar consumption (if not worse), including:

- Decreased vision and/or other eye problems
- Headaches
- Dizziness, unsteadiness
- Tinnitus (ringing in the ears)
- Depression
- Anxiety attacks
- Severe itching without a rash
- Nausea
- Abdominal pain
- Diarrhea
- Palpitations, tachycardia (rapid heart action)
- Shortness of breath
- Recent hypertension (high blood pressure)

- Atypical chest pain
- Menstrual changes
- Problems with diabetes
- Frequency of voiding (day and night), burning on urination
- Joint pains
- Excessive thirst
- Blood sugar and insulin highs and lows

Look out for names like **Aspartame, Sucralose** and **Saccharin** in foods like diet sodas, yogurts, protein powders, cereals, bars, gum, coffees and teas, flavored waters, salad dressings, baked goods, sugar-free foods.

If you have a craving for sweets, rather than trying to find "healthier" ways to continue indulging in them, why not, instead: **Permit yourself** to just eat one cookie? Add some healthy fats to your diet, as healthy fat helps to curb your sugar cravings. Or find a healthier alternative to curb your cravings, such as sipping herbal tea, taking a walk, or leaving the kitchen.

Worst case scenario: If you do reach for anything, reach for organic true green leaf stevia—a natural plant-derived natural sweetener.

Myth 10: Fruit Makes you Fat

Truth: Fruit is a real food and does not make you fat.

Many people eliminate fruit from their diets because they have been misinformed about fruit. There's a trend right now in the health and nutrition community, saying fruit sugars are harmful because of their fructose. This trend stemmed from old studies based on research using processed high fructose corn syrup, NOT NATURAL FRUCTOSE FROM FRUITS. Remember that fruits are NOT JUST SUGAR, they are carbohydrates and the cleanest burning fuel for every cell in your body.

Myth 11: If It's Organic, It's Good For You

Truth: Not all organic is created equal.

"Organic" is another one of those buzzwords that has everyone feeling like they deserve a pat on their back for making the right choice. However, organic pizza from Whole Foods is really no better than Papa John's delivery, and organic boxed cookies versus Nabisco's chocolate chip goodness are still cookies at the end of the day. Even in the produce and meat aisles, be wary of labeling—because what you see is not always what you get. Unless food is "certified organic," it may not be the real deal.

If anything, aim to buy the organic versions of the "dirty dozen" foods in the produce section as well as grass-fed, pastured and organic meats in the meat section to avoid unwanted toxins and pesticides commonly contaminated in these non-organic foods, including:

The Dirty Dozen(ish)

- Apples
- Strawberries
- Grapes
- Celery
- Peaches
- Spinach
- Sweet bell peppers
- Nectarines (imported)
- Cucumbers
- Cherry tomatoes
- Snap peas (imported)
- Potatoes
- Hot peppers
- Blueberries (domestic)

Bonus Tip: Although pastured, grass-fed and organic versions of meats may seem more expensive than the conventionally-raised Tyson or Perdue farm chicken or your generic grocery store beef, remember that we eat what our animals eat. So, if your chicken ate rat feces and was injected with antibiotics and hormones, we consume the byproducts of that. Consider your sustainable grocery choices part of your personal health care as much as you can. Don't live near a farm or have good resources and options for good quality meat, such as a local butcher, Whole Foods Market or small local natural grocer?

Check out the *http://www.eatwild.com* to find quality farmed meats close to you, or visit a national site like:

- US Wellness Meats: *http://grasslandbeef.com*
- Butcher Box: *https://www.butcherbox.com*
- Organic Prairie: *https://www.organicprairie.com*
- Greensbury: *https://www.greensbury.com*
- Vital Choice Seafood: *https://www.vitalchoice.com*

Myth 12: A Detox or Cleanse is a Great Way to Re-Wire the Body

Truth: If balanced nutrition is *not* in place first, then a cleanse forces your body to release more toxins into your body and will be unable to eliminate them.

While detoxes and cleanses most certainly can help you 'recalibrate' your body and health, "extreme" measures are not necessary or warranted to feel amazing in your skin.

A simple "cleanse" you can start today involves consistency with:

- Eating fresh, real foods—especially plenty of leafy greens and fresh veggies
- Drinking clean fresh water
- Sleeping 7-9 hours each night (to support detoxification)

- Implementing proper digestive health protocols (we will discuss)
- Throwing in a "health" hack or two, such as sipping bone broth, dry-brushing your skin, throwing out toxic beauty products or heating up some ginger herbal tea

Myth 13: Save Up for a Cheat Meal

Truth: You don't need a cheat meal

When we view food as a "cheat" or "treat" we instantly start labeling food as "good" or "bad"—therefore spurring on a silent war (inside our heads) with food—like it or not. Consequently, your "cheats" become foods that you view as "forbidden"—except, of course, on allotted cheat days or times (like post-workout, or Sunday fundays or vacation). The problem? You stay stuck in the diet mentality.

No food is morally "good" or "bad." For example, if you were to eat a Twinkie one day, **nothing** would happen.

It's what we fuel our body with consistently that matters, and if your body is used to an 80/20 balance with food—most of the time—Twinkies mean nothing for your health or body composition overall.

Myth 14: Eat 1200 Calories Every Day

Truth: Eating more—not less—calories is the way to overall health and metabolic function.

When we don't eat enough, our body goes into "reserve" mode. In reserve mode, your body reduces the number of calories expended, as well as throws off your hormonal balance in an attempt to restore energy balance.

Not knowing when it will get its next meal, and being forced to run off little fuel, your **body fights back, doing everything it can to make you stop losing calories.**

You may experience things like:

- A "sluggish" metabolism
- Hormonal imbalances
- Energy dips and highs
- Sugar, caffeine or fruit cravings
- Obsessive thoughts about food and body image
- Infertility
- Lowered immunity
  Allergies
- Bloating, constipation
- Suppressed appetite

The bottom line? Eat more—NOT less—calories for a revving metabolism (Average 1800-2200 calories as a baseline for a woman with a moderately active lifestyle—3-5 days/week of movement).

Myth 15: I Must Workout to Earn My Food

Truth: You don't have to earn it. Every single human on this planet is born with the NEED to eat food.

There's a common belief that "calories in equals calories out," and if you want to eat the foods you want, you better work for them.

Going out for pizza? Run a little longer on the treadmill.
Splurged on ice cream last night? Get your butt to the gym ASAP.
Didn't sweat today? You better watch what you eat…

Earn your food. Wrong!

Eating food is a birth-given RIGHT you have. Regardless of whether you workout, purge, deprive it to a level of extreme hunger or not, your body needs food to function. Your body does NOT see food on a gold-star cycle like you and I. It does not have to "earn" food.

Myth 16: Cookies Make You Gain Weight

Truth: There are NO innately "good" or "bad" foods.

"If I eat _____, I will gain weight."

I used to think that certain foods were automatic "answers" to either weight gain or weight loss: "If I eat salads, carrots and apples, I'll lose weight." Or, "If I eat pasta, butter or chocolate chip cookies, I'll instantly gain weight."

Listen up: **Your body is a smart cookie and does not view food on a "case-by-case" basis.**

Your body also wants to work for you—not against you—and does its best to optimize every nutrient you eat for your good (nourishment) and not at a detriment to your health. While there's a lot of talk about how "bad" sugar is for you, or how "too many carbs store as fat," or how "meat causes cancer," when we view food and "healthy eating" on a **continuum**, we realize a "little dirt never hurt" within an 80/20 balanced perspective. In other words, health is about what we eat consistently over time. One cookie won't "break" you.

Listening to Your Gut

Your gut is the gateway to your health and intuition.

Ok. We've talked about your Intuitive Heart. Knowing who you are at your core in order to be intuitive in all other areas of your life: Your Intuitive Mindset, how you think, in relation to both yourself, and also your body, specifically your relationship with food and your beliefs about food.

The last piece to reawakening our natural-born intuition and food relationship is physical, and it starts in our gut.

Your gut is the *foundation* upon which ALL other systems of the body are found healthy or unhealthy—including your mental health, your immune system, cardiovascular system, thyroid and endocrine system (hormones), and every other cell in your body from head to toe.

Think about it. What other body system is responsible for processing and directing all the life-giving nutrients and fuel you give it throughout your lifetime, as well as detoxing any pollutants or toxins?

Your gut and digestive system.

Fun Facts:

- **80% of your immune cells** are housed in your digestive system—your gut.

- **90-95% of your serotonin** (your "feel good" mood-boosting chemicals) are produced in your gut.

- The microbiome is now **considered an endocrine organ**: it controls the production of hormones, and inhibits or support hormonal balance.

- Only 1 in 2 people report digestive issues like constipation, diarrhea, gas before diagnosis, yet **an estimated 75% of all Americans struggle with some sort of GI dysfunction.**

In other words, your gut health has more to do with your body than simply feeling bloated after meals.

And, if you do have "gut issues," you don't always feel the effects of digestive distress in your stomach. Examples include colds, illness, low mood, obsessive or distracted thinking, hormone imbalances, and more.

This is why when we're talking about "going with your gut" or reawakening your intuition, we must address the health of your gut and re-wiring your health and body's natural cues from there.

What does an "unhealthy" gut look like? Some signs and symptoms of an unhealthy gut include:

- Low stomach acid and bloating after meals
- IBS or loose stools
- Bacterial overgrowth (SIBO) or parasites
- Celiac disease and autoimmune conditions
- Lowered immunity and sickness
- Feelings of anxiety or depression
- Autoimmune conditions
- Brittle nails
- Thinning hair
- Fatigue
- Feelings of cold
- Popping or clicking joints
- Frequent headaches
- Hypermetabolic or sluggish metabolism
- Crazy sugar or caffeine cravings (because you're not absorbing your nutrients)
- Seasonal allergies
- Low libido or hormone imbalances
- Nutrient deficiencies and electrolyte imbalances
- Poor focus/concentration and ADD/ADHD
- Acne and skin breakouts
- Osteoporosis
- And a wide range of other diseases, including diabetes, obesity, rheumatoid arthritis, autism spectrum disorder, depression, and chronic fatigue syndrome.

How does your gut (and consequently your brain, your stress levels and intuition) become imbalanced in the first place?

Digestive "issues" or gut imbalances stem from some reasons, including:

- Undigested food and poor digestive practices (eating fast, not chewing your food well)
- Toxins, such as environmental cleaning products, fumes, hygiene products, smoking, and excessive alcohol consumption
- Not chewing your food well or eating too fast
- Long-term use of some medications
- Lack of zinc (a critical mineral for gut lining health)
- Birth history (C-section or not breastfeeding) and family medical history
- Eating disorder rituals (binging, purging, restricting)
- Stress (physical, mental, emotional)
- Inflammation (parasites, low stomach acid, bacterial overgrowth, yeast)
- Over-exercising or sedentary lifestyles
- Running off coffee
- Insatiable sweet tooth
- Lack of water
- Fake food like Pop-tarts and Goldfish you ate as a child
- Liver dysfunction (like from a low-fat diet)
- Bacterial overgrowth (from lack of "good bacteria" in your gut)
- Consumption of hydrogenated oils, sugar, trans fats, conventional meats and dairy, processed grains and diet foods—like Lean Cuisines, Splenda, Quest Bars or Special K Cereal
- Food poisoning
- Sleep deprivation
- Stress (especially chronic)
- Hypothyroidism/Hyperthyroidism
- Low stomach acid (stomach acid HELPS you digest)

If you are not living in a bubble, the cards are stacked against you to struggle with gut health, and there is often a handful of reasons why your gut health goes south.

These signs and symptoms are a far cry from how your normal process of digestion should work.

In an ideal world, "good digestion" would look something like this:

- Chewing your food thoroughly and breaking it down before you swallow.
- Full digestion through the digestive tract (approximately 6-8 hours in the small intestine, where nutrients are delivered throughout the body)
- Regular, well-formed sausage-like poops one to three times per day (every day)
- Rare gas, constipation, nausea, stomach cramps or pains, or heartburn around meals
- Regular appetite
- No extreme fullness after meals
- No allergies (environmental or food)
- Clear skin
- Energy throughout the day
- Low/no nutritional deficiencies
- Low/no headaches
- Healthy immune system (rarely sick)
- No strong cravings (for sweets or caffeine)
- Low anxiety and uncontrollable thoughts
- Not obsessing or stressing about food or your body

All organs and systems are functioning at their peak within the healthy digestive process.

Intuitive Digestion

Good digestion is imperative for intuitive eating.

If your gut is **unable** to effectively or efficiently digest your food and absorb your nutrients for all your body systems, create serotonin and balance brain cells and chemicals, or fight disease, inflammation and stress, then you will continue to miss the mark in your ability to *truly* be "more intuitive" and *listen* to your body's real cues.

For example, did you know that sometimes cravings for certain foods (even if they tend to make us bloated or gassy) are actually our gut bugs and fermenting bacteria in our gut demanding more foods? Many theories about intuitive eating and food cravings will tell you that food cravings are only "in your head," or related to emotional eating. However, we actually often "intuitively" crave foods we are intolerant to— continuing to eat the cookies, sandwich bread, peanut butter, or cheese as we not only feed ourselves, but the trillions of bacteria housed in our guts—particularly the unhealthy gut bacteria when such cravings strike.

Similarly, for those who struggle with a loss of appetite, under-eating (not necessarily dieting) or rarely feeling hungry, this could also be about more than simply not wanting to eat. Your body needs adequate stomach acid and digestive enzymes to break down foods in the first place. When it is low in stomach acid and/or enzymes, "intuitively" we may **not** feel hungry—even though our body is not nourished.

And, did you know that blood sugar dips—like that 3 p.m. wall you hit when your body cries out for caffeine or sugar, or often experiencing hunger every two to three hours between meals—are actually signs that you may not be digesting foods to sustain our energy? If your gut is unable to effectively *absorb* nutrients or if you have a "leaky gut" (an irritated gut lining that leaks undigested food into your bloodstream), then your cells do not get adequately nourished. This disrupts intuitive eating skills, making us think our sugar or caffeine fix will supply us with energy, only to crave something to eat again shortly after.

This is why healing your relationship with food and your body is about **more** than simply declaring peace with cupcakes on your birthday, practicing mind-over-matter, fighting off cravings, dealing with emotional eating, or self-affirmations.

You can read all the motivational self-help and intuitive eating books in the world, focus on mentally managing stress and emotions, and try to use willpower to overcome cravings, but if there is still a disconnect in your gut, your brain (and your ability to go with your gut) may lag behind.

So…How is Your Digestion?

"Ok, ok, ok. I hear you. So how do I KNOW if I have a "gut imbalance?" you ask.

Simple.

Check in with yourself: **How do you feel?**

Knowledge is power.

Here are some common signs and symptoms that hint at imbalances in various body systems that are connected (ultimately) to your gut health and nourishing food choices (*adapted from "Signs and Symptoms Analysis from a Functional Perspective" by Dicken Weatherby*).

Scoring
Count one for each symptom you possess and keep count for each category individually (0=no, 1=yes). Add up your numbers within each section.

0-8 = Low priority
9-13 = Moderate Priority
14-19+ = High Priority

High Priority areas point to the regions of your body most sensitive to imbalance. This screening tool can help you (and/or your practitioner) get a clearer picture of where to start with lab testing or digging deeper.

Upper GI

- ☐ Belching, bloating or gas within one hour of eating
- ☐ Heartburn or acid reflux
- ☐ Bad breath (halitosis)
- ☐ Loss of taste for meat
- ☐ Strong odor in sweat
- ☐ Sense of excess fullness after meals
- ☐ Stomach upset by taking vitamins
- ☐ Sleepy after meals
- ☐ Diarrhea, chronic or after meals
- ☐ Undigested food in stools
- ☐ Fingernails chip, peel or break easily
- ☐ Anemia (iron deficiency)
- ☐ Stomach pains or cramps
- ☐ Feel better if you don't eat
- ☐ Vegan diet

Small Intestine

- ☐ Dairy sensitivity
- ☐ Food allergies
- ☐ Airborne allergies
- ☐ Crave bread or noodles or starchy carbs and fruits
- ☐ Alternating constipation or diarrhea

- ☐ Wheat or grain sensitivity
- ☐ Pulse speeds up after eating
- ☐ Feel spacey
- ☐ Get hives
- ☐ Sinus congestion/stuffy head
- ☐ Bizarre vivid dreams/nightmares
- ☐ Use of over-the-counter meds

Large Intestine

- ☐ Dark circles under eyes
- ☐ Anus itch
- ☐ Stools are not well-formed
- ☐ Mucus in stool
- ☐ Foul smelling lower bowel gas
- ☐ Cramping in lower abdomen
- ☐ Stools are hard or difficult to pass
- ☐ Less than one bowel movement per day
- ☐ Fungus or yeast infections
- ☐ Taking an antibiotic for a long period of time
- ☐ Feel worse in moldy places
- ☐ Coated tongue
- ☐ Irritable bowel or mucus colitis
- ☐ Stools have corners or edges that are flattened or ribbon shaped
- ☐ Painful to press long outside of thighs (IT Band)
- ☐ History of parasites
- ☐ Ringworm, jock itch, athletes foot or nail fungus

Liver/Gallbladder

- ☐ Pain between shoulder blades
- ☐ Sensitive to chemicals (perfume, cleaning agents)
- ☐ History of drug/alcohol use

- ☐ Easily sick, intoxicated or hungover if you drink wine
- ☐ Gallbladder attacks
- ☐ Headache over eyes
- ☐ Dry skin, itchy feet or skin peels on feet
- ☐ Motion sickness
- ☐ Nausea
- ☐ Greasy or shiny stools
- ☐ Stomach easily upset by fats
- ☐ Bitter taste in mouth after meals
- ☐ Light, clay colored stools
- ☐ Chronic fatigue or Fibromyalgia
- ☐ Nutrasweet (aspartame) consumption
- ☐ Sensitivity to aspartame
- ☐ Pain under right side of rib cage
- ☐ History of hepatitis
- ☐ Significant alcohol consumption

Mineral Needs

- ☐ History of carpal tunnel
- ☐ History of lower right abdominal pains or ileocecal valve problems
- ☐ History of stress fracture
- ☐ Bone loss on a bone scale
- ☐ Herniated disc
- ☐ Morning stiffness
- ☐ Crave chocolate
- ☐ History of anemia
- ☐ Hoarseness
- ☐ Lump in throat
- ☐ Difficulty swallowing/dry mouth and/or nose
- ☐ Cold sores/fever blisters

- ☐ Frequent skin rashes
- ☐ Muscle cramps at rest
- ☐ History of stress fractures or bone loss
- ☐ Bursitis/Tendonitis
- ☐ Clicking or popping joints
- ☐ Swelling joints
- ☐ Gag easily
- ☐ Lump in throat
- ☐ Dry mouth/eyes/nose
- ☐ White of eyes is blue tinted
- ☐ Cuts heal slowly or scar easily
- ☐ Decreased sense of taste or smell
- ☐ White spots on fingernails
- ☐ Difficulty swallowing
- ☐ Morning stiffness
- ☐ History of bone spurs
- ☐ Feet have a strong odor

Essential Fatty Acid Deficiencies

- ☐ Experience pain relief with aspirin
- ☐ Crave fatty or greasy food
- ☐ Tension headaches
- ☐ Tension at base of skull
- ☐ Headaches when out in the sun
- ☐ Muscles easily fatigued
- ☐ Low-or reduced-fat diet (current or history)
- ☐ Sunburn easily
- ☐ Dry flaky skin or dandruff

Sugar Handling

- ☐ Awaken a few hours after falling asleep

- ❏ Crave sweets
- ❏ Binge or uncontrolled appetite
- ❏ Sleepy in the afternoon
- ❏ Crave coffee or sugar
- ❏ Fatigue that is relieved by eating
- ❏ Frequent thirst or urination
- ❏ Family with diabetes
- ❏ Shaky if meals are delayed
- ❏ Irritable before meals
- ❏ Headache is meals are skipped

Vitamin Deficiencies

- ❏ Racing heart
- ❏ Depressed
- ❏ Muscles easily fatigued
- ❏ Feel sore after moderate exercise
- ❏ Pulse below 65 beats per minute
- ❏ Ringing in ears
- ❏ Numbness or tingling in hands/feet
- ❏ Worrier or anxious
- ❏ Night sweats
- ❏ Restless leg syndrome
- ❏ Nose bleeds/easily bruise
- ❏ Small bumps on back of arms
- ❏ MSG sensitivity
- ❏ Bleeding gums when brushing teeth
- ❏ Cracks in corners of mouth
- ❏ Whole body limb jerk as falling asleep
- ❏ Polyps or warts
- ❏ Can hear heart beat on pillow at night
- ❏ Loss of muscle tone/heaviness in arms

❐ Nervous or agitated
❐ Feeling insecure
❐ Vulnerable to insect bites

Adrenal (Stress Hormones) Imbalances

❐ Tend to be a "night person"
❐ Difficulty falling asleep
❐ Slow starter in the morning
❐ Blood pressure above 120/80
❐ Anxiety
❐ Headache after exercise
❐ Clench or grind teeth
❐ Feel wired or jittery after drinking coffee
❐ Become dizzy when standing up suddenly
❐ Chronic fatigue
❐ Sweat easily
❐ Crave salty foods
❐ Arthritic tendencies
❐ Allergies
❐ Weakness, dizziness
❐ Tendency to sprain ankles/shin splints
❐ Afternoon yawning/headache
❐ Salt foods before tasting
❐ Chronic low back pain
❐ Calm on the outside, troubled on the inside
❐ Pain after manipulative correction
❐ Perspire easily
❐ Pain on medial or inner side of knee
❐ Difficulty maintaining manipulative correction

Thyroid

❐ Difficulty gaining **or** losing weight (one or the other)

- ☐ Constipation
- ☐ Seasonal sadness
- ☐ Loss of lateral 1/3 of eyebrow
- ☐ Excessive hair loss
- ☐ Mentally sluggish
- ☐ Easily fatigued
- ☐ Fast pulse rate while at rest
- ☐ Inward trembling
- ☐ Nervous, emotional
- ☐ Difficulty working under pressure
- ☐ Sensitive/allergic to iodine
- ☐ Seasonal sadness
- ☐ Reduced initiative
- ☐ Sensitive to cold/poor circulation in hands or feet
- ☐ Nervous or emotional/can't work under pressure
- ☐ Intolerance to high temperatures
- ☐ Flush early

Hormonal Imbalance

- ☐ Depression during periods
- ☐ Mood swings associated with period (PMS)
- ☐ Crave chocolate during periods
- ☐ Breast tenderness with cycle
- ☐ Excessive menstrual flow
- ☐ Scanty blood flow during periods
- ☐ Occasional skipped periods
- ☐ Variations in menstrual cycles
- ☐ Endometriosis
- ☐ Uterine fibroids
- ☐ Breast fibroids
- ☐ Pain with intercourse
- ☐ Vaginal discharge

❏ Vaginal dryness
❏ Vaginal itching
❏ Gain weight around hips, thighs and buttocks
❏ Excess facial or body hair
❏ Hot flashes
❏ Night sweats (in menopausal females)
❏ Thinning skin

Immune System

❏ Runny drippy nose
❏ Catch colds at the beginning of winter
❏ Mucus cough
❏ Acne
❏ Itchy Skin
❏ Never get sick (0=sick only 1-2 times in last 2 years, 1=not sick in last 2 years, 2=not sick in last 4 years, 3=not sick in last 7 years)
❏ Other infections (sinus, ear, lung, skin, bladder, kidney, etc.)
❏ Frequent colds/flu
❏ Cysts, boils or rashes
❏ History of Epstein Bar, Mono, Herpes, Shingles, Chronic Fatigue Syndrome, Hepatitis, or other chronic viral condition (0=no, 1=yes, in the past, 2=currently a mild condition, 3=severe)

Healing Your Gut & Reawakening Gut Intuition

"Oh man...I didn't realize how much the gut influences health! How do I heal (and love) my gut if it IS imbalanced?"

No sweat! I've got your back.

Let's discuss the best practices of all for both healing and listening to your gut, including **reawakening your intuitive physical abilities** to compliment the head and heart work we talked about earlier and **rewiring your gut and body** for optimal intuitive health and function.

The practices for **reawakening** your "intuitive gut" include:

- **Eating real foods** which your body was meant to thrive upon

- Incorporating **healthy digestive wellness** into your daily life-style (i.e. chewing your food well, slowing down at meals, pro-biotics, and fermented foods)

- **Primal movement** like exercising and moving how your body was wired to move

- **Cultivating the basics of self care** like sleep and addressing stress

- And, ultimately, cultivating intuitive and mindful eating aware-ness with our one primary check-in question: ***"How do I feel?"***

Reawakening Gut Intuition: Eat Real Food

Good Nutrition in 100 words:

Eat real food—as close to its natural state as possible. If it didn't grow on the land, roam the earth, or swim in the sea, it's not real food. Meat and fish. Healthy fats. Veggies. Fruits. Some starch. No added sugar. Lots of water. Support local, responsible producers. Food is not about perfection. Keep an 80/20 balance with both food and life. Let life happen. When in Rome, eat pasta. Enjoy your birthday cake. Don't let fear of food keep you from all that life has to offer. Above all, ditch the obsessive diet mentality and question conventional wisdom.

The simplest formula to reawaken your gut (body) intuition starts with food. Real food. No, not necessarily raw, vegan, paleo, or diet foods. Real food doesn't have a label or diet rules. Long before stereotypes, diet ads, or nutrition bars branded as "gluten-free," "paleo" or "sugar-free," real food was all that humans knew.

Real food (noun): If you can't pick it, grow it or kill it, more than likely it's not real food.

Think about it: Foods you would have eaten had you been born 3000 years ago. A balance of fresh, simple, one-ingredient foods, including meat, poultry and fish, colorful veggies and fruits, nuts and seeds, and healthy oils and fats (such as coconut oil, ghee, extra virgin olive oil and avocado).

A Lesson in Gut Intuition from Cats

When we eat real food (and silence the food rules in our heads), we answer our body's deepest calling to thrive.

Dr. Pottenger's famous **cat study** was the first of its kind to prove the impact that real food has on our health and body's natural intuitive design.

Over the course of 10 years, Pottenger studied and tested the effects of the consumption of 'living food' (ie. raw meat, cod liver oil, and raw milk) versus 'dead food' (i.e. foods resembling our modern day processed, packaged, diet foods) in over 700 cats—three generations worth. Over time, he found that cats who ate a natural raw diet, consisting of real foods lived healthier lives and produced healthier offspring (in all three generations), than the cats who ate processed, pasteurized and cooked foods.

The cats who were fed raw milk and meat were more agile, energetic and strong, had increased sexual interest (well-functioning hormones), fully developed skills and abilities (like jumping high), aged better, and had a shinier coat, than compared to the cats fed the "fake food" diet. Although the "fake food" cats fed and gave birth to healthy appearing offspring in the first generation, the offspring cats developed diseases and illnesses near the end of their lives.

The processed-food cats were also, generally more lethargic, anxious and uncoordinated, had dental deterioration, arthritis, smaller skulls, and greater bodily deterioration (ie. lung failure, enlargement of the liver, etc.). In fact, they were unable to reproduce by the third generation altogether.

Near the conclusion of the 10-year study, the last experiment was conducted on this unhealthy third generation. Pottenger fed these cats the same raw food diet that had been fed to the control group of cats to see what would happen. The conclusion? Restoration. Pottenger found that it took about four generations of the cats eating a raw food diet for the first offspring to be born normal and healthy.

Results from this study imply what we eat matters to support our body, intuition, and mind.

Disconnected Cultural Norms

It's pretty crazy how far our society has gotten away from real food. In fact, 80% of the foods found in the grocery store is packaged and processed. Granola bars, cereals, yogurts, processed cheese, enriched bread, fortified juices, frozen dinners, diet sodas and beyond, we have all encountered the SAD diet (Standard American Diet) at some point in our lives.

What's the big deal about eating these "fake foods"—especially the ones labeled gluten-free, heart-healthy, or sugar-free, though?

Chemicals and additives found in man-made foods are linked to a host of symptoms and side effects like inflammation, blood sugar and hormonal imbalances, low energy, allergies, chronic disease (autoimmune, cancer, mental health disease, hypo/hyperthyroid), and poor gut health (yup, back to square one).

What we eat matters, not because it "makes us fat" or "lazy" or mentally weak, but because we disrupt our own gut intuition.

Of course, this doesn't mean you have to drop everything to go live in Amish country or a teepee on the open range. Nor does it mean becoming "orthorexic" and obsessing over the righteousness or quality of everything you put in your mouth.

What it does mean is when you stick to eating real foods, **most** of the time (80/20 balance) and love your gut with some extra special care, no food is off limits and you will thrive—from the inside out for your best health!

The BEST part?

No other "old rules" for eating apply! I'm talking:

NO counting calories

NO weighing and measuring your food

NO calculating how many carbs, or protein grams, or fat you've consumed

NO My Fitness Pal app

Out with the old, in with the new. Here are the basics you need to know about "real food" —part of your "Redefined" nutrition blueprint:

Reawakening Gut Intuition with Real Food: Water

Water is the single most important nutrient you can consume on a daily basis. And more than likely, you are not drinking enough.

How much water do I need to drink? Half your bodyweight in ounces is the general prescription "starting point" for the average person engaging in normal activities of daily living. Add in factors such as your physical activity and workouts, the heat or humidity in your climate, and your water needs may increase.

Why so much water? *Every* function of the body is monitored and conducted by the flow of water. Your body alone is comprised of 60-80% water (fluid) itself, so to be "lively" it *needs water*. Water ensures that adequate amounts of nutrients reach your organs, your food is digested properly, your brain thinks clearly, your metabolism is functioning adequately (ie. energy), your cells regenerate and your body overcomes daily stressors, and more.

Side Effects of Dehydration:

- **Decreased energy.** Everything moves slower when we lack water (including your metabolic function).

- **Digestive dysfunction:** Constipation, bloating, indigestion, GERD, leaky gut, abdominal discomfort.

- **Chronic pain**. Ailments such as headaches, back pain, neck pain, heartburn, rheumatoid pain, high blood pressure, high cholesterol, chest pains, allergies and asthma can all be directly attributed to a water shortage in your body.

- **Depression and stress.** Since your brain is made up of 75% water, it needs water to continue to flourish and for your chemical properties to work correctly. With dehydration, the level of energy generation in the brain is decreased.

- **Morning sickness.** A woman often experiences this during pregnancy and it can actually be a thirst signal of her body and the fetus.' In addition, if you wake up nauseous or not hungry in the morning, consider your body's need to replenish with water.

Water Drinking Tips:

1. **Don't rely on thirst.** Thirst or dry mouth is the 'final straw' when it comes to your body signaling, "I need water." Translation: Your body needs plenty of water before you hit this breaking point. Make sure to sip up throughout the day so you never go over the edge.

2. **Hunger confusion.** Often, a growling stomach or hunger pangs are a sign of your body's cry for water! Why? Hunger and thirst signals are controlled in the same part of your brain (the hypothalamus). The next time hunger strikes, ask yourself how much water you have had that day.

3. **Keep it with you.** A quality BPA-free, stainless-steel water bottle is a great way to stay hydrated throughout the day. Opt to fill it with filtered water (not tap water) as often as you can. Environmental pollutants are hard to regulate and extract from our tap water sources—particularly lead, mercury, arsenic, radon, and nitrates. Purchasing a water filter for your home is a small investment with a large return for your health.

4. **Start your day off right.** Aim to drink 16-ounces of your water for the day upon waking. Why? Your body is thirsty! After about 6-8 hours of working to recover and restore your metabolic processes, your tissue repair and reset your batteries for a brand new day.

5. **Around Meals.** Typically, it's not recommended to drink water during meals so as not to conflict with your stomach acid for optimal digestion. Cap your water intake then to about 20-30 minutes before a meal, and 20-30 minutes after meals. Sip, don't chug.

Reawakening Gut Intuition with Real Food: Protein

Protein is essential for the making up the skeletal structure of all your cells, hence why it is called the **"basic building block" of nutrition**. Protein is the **only macronutrient** which comprises all 22 naturally occurring amino acids that your body needs for:

- Metabolic function (regulating energy and all the cellular processes)
- Building and repairing muscle
- The contraction of your muscles (ability to use them)
- Transporting oxygen, nutrients and waste throughout the body
- Composing your body structures (bones, hair, nails, skin, organs, etc.).

Protein is also the most satiating of all macronutrients. Once you've digested it, complete proteins send signals to your brain, telling you to stop eating—you are full and nourished.

While every food on this planet has some bit of protein in it, the optimal sources of protein are those with the complete amino acid profile, including:

- Meat (grass-fed beef, bison)

- Poultry (chicken, turkey, hen)
- Pasture-raised eggs
- Organ meat
- Wild game (reindeer, venison, rabbit, alligator, emu, elk, kangaroo, buffalo)
- Duck, quail, pheasant
- Lamb
- Pastured pork
- Wild-caught fish and seafood
- Organic, nitrate-free deli meats, bacon, sausage

How much do I need?

The daily baseline requirements for protein are at least 0.5 grams per pound of body weight. However, counting grams is not necessary. Just have a protein source with every meal for meal balance. An adequate serving size of protein is approximately the sizes of one to two palms of your hand at most meals, about one-fourth to one-third of of plate. For athletes and active individuals, this increases slightly. Just remember that protein is an essential component of muscle strengthening, tone, firing and performance, as well as mental clarity, energy and satiation during and between meals.

What happens if I do not eat enough protein?

Too little protein in the diet limits the amount of protein your body can use for daily cell function and building muscle.

What happens if I eat too much protein?

A diet containing excess protein can lead to digestive disturbances, especially if you are not consuming fats or carbs (especially veggies) and drinking water throughout the day. Also, the body will store some excess for future energy.

Doesn't meat cause cancer?

Poor quality, hormone-injected and sick meat can cause inflammation and has been linked to diseases like cancer. Avoid processed soy, farmed seafood, pasteurized milk, cheap eggs, conventional or grain-fed meats, and processed conventional meats with nitrates (deli meat, bacon, Spam, frozen dinners).

But isn't organic meat more expensive?

Opt for organic, grass-fed and/or pastured meats as much as possible to avoid unknown hormones and poor quality food sources your animals may have ingested. However, if choosing non-organic, buy leaner versions of those meats since the majority of toxins in poor quality meat are stored in the animal fat. Also, stock up when you find grass-fed or pastured meats on sale and store it in your freezer, as well as look in the frozen meat section or connect with a local farmer at a farmer's market for potential better deals.

How about protein shakes?

They aren't *necessary*—particularly for the average gym-goer, whose main objective is to look good naked. However, protein powder can be a great addition to add to a smoothie or quick snack. If you do choose a protein powder, less is more regarding ingredients. Aim for brands without artificial sweeteners and additives with names you cannot pronounce. Collagen Peptides, beef isolates, bone broth protein and hemp protein with short ingredient lists are generally the best digesting formulas.

What if I am vegan or vegetarian?

There are protein options if you are a vegetarian or vegan, but it is important you remain conscious and make an effort to get in your daily needs, particularly Zinc, B-Vitamins and digestive support, including enzymes, probiotics and hydrochloric acid to absorb your nutrients in the first place. Depending on your personal plant-based lifestyle, some good vegetarian and vegan sources may include pastured eggs, fish, tuna, presoaked beans and nuts, hemp protein powder and other additive-free powders (see above), bone broth, full-fat grass-fed plain dairy sources, seeds and fermented natural soy (miso, tempeh, natto). However, "incomplete" proteins, like rice and beans, nuts, quinoa, or even broccoli and other greens, are secondary sources, compared to fish, dairy, natural soy and egg sources.

Reawakening Gut Intuition with Real Food: Healthy Fats

Eating fat does not make you fat. In fact, it does the opposite: It boosts metabolism, prevents fat storage, aids in digestion and gives you more energy, brain power and clarity to think intuitively.

Get the facts. **What is fat?**

- **Fats are made of long-chain fatty acids that compose the outside structure of our cells**—they are responsible for letting nutrients, toxins, sugar and more in and out of our cells.

- Fat is the **densest source of energy** we consume. From a calorie standpoint, there are nine calories for every 1 gram of fat, as opposed to 4 calories for every gram of protein or carbohydrate.

Why Do We Fear Fat So Much?

NPR traces Americans' fear of fat to July 1976, when Senator George McGovern called an urgent hearing to raise attention to the links between diet and disease. This hearing was spurred on by an increase in Senate member deaths at the time (8 total during the 1960's and 70's).

Sen. McGovern and others tried to explain the outbreak. With few answers, they concluded that Americans "must be eating too much fat," based on a few early studies scientists had been conducting on saturated fat (like eggs and meat). The idea stuck, and what began as a discussion spread like wildfire. By 1977, the USDA released its first set of Dietary Goals, warning Americans against the consumption of fats and oils, while emphasizing the consumption of grains, fruit, dairy, veggies and some protein, and saying nothing about sugar.

The primary belief of the era was that eating fat makes you fat and unhealthy. Enter: *The War Against Fat.*

Ironically, during this time of fat-fear as Americans began to avoid foods with fat, eat less red meat and full-fat dairy, and increase their intake of grains, corn, sugar and high-fructose corn syrup, the obesity epidemic also began (recorded as early as 1976). By the 1990s, the majority of TV marketing, grocery-store shelves, and American consumers were "all aboard" the Low-Fat Belief System (bring on the Slim Fast, Kashi Go Lean and Special K cereals, Lean Cuisines, dry green salads and reduced-fat versions of everything from peanut butter to salad dressings, ice cream and bread).

To date, although more and more Americans have heard "Fat is not the enemy," many still fear fat. Repeat after me: **Fat does not make you fat.**

Benefits of Fat:

- **Energy:** Fat is the densest source of energy we consume great for many things, like the below!

- **Optimal Brain Function.** Your brain is composed of 60% fat and cholesterol, and for peak functioning you need to eat fats to develop, sustain, and promote brain power.

- **Cholesterol.** Your body needs cholesterol to function. If you had zero cholesterol in your body you would not exist. No cells, no bone structure, no muscles, no hormones, no sex, no reproductive system, no digestion, no brain function, no memory, no nerve endings, no movement, no human life – nothing without cholesterol. Even better? Higher cholesterol levels appear to improve memory and cognitive skills and protect against neurodegenerative diseases such as Alzheimer's, while low blood cholesterol is associated with poor cognitive performance.

- **Healthy Digestion.** Healthy fats assist the digestion of your food through your system thanks to their fat-soluble vitamins. Fat also helps your body produce bile, which is essential for elimination and proper digestion.

- **Helps Absorb All Your Vitamins & Nutrients.** You've probably heard Vitamin D is good for building strong bones and energy. You need Vitamin A for good vision and healthy skin. Vitamin E helps with wound healing and Vitamin K is necessary for blood clotting. These vitamins are known as "fat soluble" vitamins, and to actually work, they need fats. Fats help transport these vitamins to where they are needed.

- **Produces & Supports Hormones.** Fat is essential for reproductive health. Our hormones are built from fat. Chances are if your hormones are out of whack, your fatty acids are out of whack too, leading to low libido, amenorrhea, irregular cycles, poor strength gains and recovery from exercise, moodiness and more.

- **Boosts your Metabolism.** Eat fat for a revving metabolism and to potentially even burn fat. Healthy fats in your diet help trigger hormones that release fat, and eliminate toxins that make it hard for your body to otherwise have a fiery metabolism or shed unwanted pounds.

- **Healthy Skin, Hair & Tissues.** Dry skin, hair, and eyes, and thin nails all are directly attributed to fatty acid deficiencies. Fat soluble vitamins (A, D, K, E) help keep skin aglow.

- **Satiates You & Staves Off Hunger.** Fats help you feel satisfied and keep you feeling full for longer.

- **Stronger Immunity**. Saturated fats (i.e. butter, coconut oil, and red palm oil) contain the fatty acids lauric and myristic acid. These are anti-microbial, anti-viral, and anti-fungal, with the ability to decrease infection rates by killing bacteria such as harmful candida yeast.

- **It Tastes Good.** No questions about it, **fat makes everything taste better!** Drizzle on the olive oil, spread with coconut butter or grass-fed butter, saute in ghee, slice up some avocado, fry up some sunny-side-up eggs with nitrate-free bacon, sprinkle olives or pecans on your salad, crust your fish with coconut flakes, add that full-fat organic creamer to your coffee.

How Much Fat Do I Need?

Have no fear. Incorporate one to two healthy fats with each of your main meals (at least three times per day). A serving is generally a spoonful (tablespoon) of oil, butter, coconut butter or nut butter; half an avocado; or a closed handful of nuts, seeds, or olives. If cravings or hunger strikes between meals, reach for a fat or protein-based snack to help curb blood sugar dips and keep cravings at bay.

Best Sources of Fat? Select from any of the following:

- Raw nuts & seeds
- Nut butter (almond, cashew, walnut, pecan)
- Sunflower seed butter (unsweetened, unsalted)
- Olives, Extra virgin olive oil
- Coconut Butter, Coconut Oil, Coconut flakes
- Grass-fed butter or Ghee
- Nitrate free bacon
- Raw almond flour/meal
- Full-fat raw dairy (milk, cheese, yogurt)
- Avocado, Avocado oil, Avocado oil mayo
- Nut oils (walnut, almond, hazelnut)
- Tallow, Lard, Duck fat
- Pastured egg yolks
- Grass-fed, pastured animal meats (beef, bison, chicken, turkey)
- Wild-caught fatty fish (salmon, halibut, tuna)
- Cod liver oil/Fish oil (take 1-2 x daily)

Reawakening Gut Intuition with Real Food: Carbs

Similar to the "fat scare," carbs have been a long-time hot topic since the early 90's (1992) when Dr. Atkins' released his updated diet book: *The Atkins' Diet* and Americans were swept away into the next big diet fad of low carb.

So, are carbs really necessary? Before we answer that question, let's define: **What is a carb?**

Carbs 101

Carbohydrates are macronutrients which are your body's easiest, quickest go-to source of energy. This energy is derived from the sugar, starch and/or fiber in each molecule—ranging from simple to more complex, depending on the type of food it is. Carbohydrates all contain glucose (i.e. "energy") and our brains, muscle tissue, and cells, require carbohydrates to keep going and do just about anything, such as build lean muscle, be in the optimal body for you, pass your anatomy test, balance your hormones, keep your metabolism revving, and more.

Types of Carbs. There are multiple forms of carbohydrates, including:

- Vegetables (greens, broccoli, zucchini, asparagus, cauliflower, green beans, Brussels sprouts)
- Fresh fruits
- Starches (potatoes, sweet potatoes, winter squash, parsnips, beets, carrots)
- Grains (rice, oats, corn, quinoa, couscous)
- Sweets & Treats (cookies, honey, syrup, candy bars)
- Refined Foods (packaged granola bars, chips, graham crackers,)

Benefits of Carbs:

- Promote lean muscle building, especially when paired with protein
- Enhance digestion (especially fibrous, leafy greens)
- Quick source of energy
- Hormone balance
- Brain function & Mental sanity (keep from going into 'no carb' crazy)

Roadblocks with Carbs

As with anything, too much of a "good thing" is not always a good thing. Some common side effects when we are not intuitive and eat less real-food carbs (and more processed food carbs) include:

- **High Sugar Consumption.** Some carbs have more sugar than others—particularly refined foods, sweets and tropical fruits. When the body gets too much sugar, it experiences a quick spike in energy followed by a crash.
- **Grain Brain.** An excess of grains can lead to brain fog and decreased mental clarity and focus.
- **Poor Digestion & Leaky Gut.** While leafy greens, veggies and some starchy carbs like sweet potatoes and beets can promote enhanced digestion, poor quality sources of carbs—like processed refined foods or gluten-containing foods—can be difficult to digest.

Survey Says

Although low carb has been all the rage in the modern day, you still need carbs for energy, no questions asked! Incorporate color into your plate with carbohydrates! Rich orange sweet potatoes, ruby red strawberries, navy blue blueberries, forest green kale, spinach and zucchini, green asparagus, rich maroon beets—you name it, there's a Crayola crayon name for that!

How Many Do I Need?

For the average person, roughly 30 - 40% of our diets should come from carbs, with the majority of those being plants, like low-sugar veggies and real-food starches. If you look at your plate, about half of it should be made of veggies—at least one to two at each meal. Aim to eat a serving or two of leafy greens each day, along with any other fibrous veggies of choice, one or two starchy veggies and tubers, and one or two fresh fruits.

How about grams? Again, no counting is necessary. Your body doesn't calculate food like the MyFitnessPal app, and since every body is different, different amounts of carbs, proteins and fats will vary (even daily). Some days you may recognize you eat more carbohydrate, and less protein. Other days, you may notice you have a little more fat than carbs. The yin and the yang are what balance is all about. Above all: Ask yourself (and your gut), "How do I feel?"

Optimal sources of carbs include vegetables, 1-3 servings of fruits, and legumes/grains. In the next chapter, we will discuss your Nutrition Blueprint and go over in detail what foods will best serve you.

Reawakening Your Gut Intuition: Nutrition Blueprint

By incorporating real foods at the foundation of what you eat, you will learn how to fuel your body for life and how to LISTEN to it again, instead of simply telling you how many calories to eat or giving you macronutrient prescriptions.

Your basic blueprint for optimal nutrition is based on REAL foods your body recognizes:

- Meat and fish
- Plenty of healthy fats (plant and animal fats)
- Vegetables
- Some fruit and starchy veggies
- Minimal (added) sugar
- Lots of water
- Lots of colorful veggies
- Fresh herbs and spices
- Gut-healing and nourishing foods (Fermented Foods, Bone Broth)
- And, occasionally, chocolate or mom's homemade spaghetti

The _one_ philosophy? Be Nourished.

Eating is NOT about rules, and when we eat real foods our body was meant to thrive upon, it does a pretty darn good job of figuring out "what to do" with the food we eat and tell you what it needs.

Here is an example of a Daily Fuel Template you can use as a starting point:

Water: ½ bodyweight in ounces minimum/daily

Pre-Breakfast:

- 12-16 oz. warm water with lemon & sea salt
- Probiotic supplement or fermented food (Medicinal dose: ex. sauerkraut-2-3 forkfuls, water kefir, or 2-4 oz. kombucha)

Breakfast:

- Protein - 5-6 ounces (1-2 hand sizes)
- Veggies - Approximately half a plate
- Fat - 1-2 sources (1 Tbsp avocado oil/olive oil/butter/ghee/ nut butter, ½ avocado, fistful of nuts, etc. = 1 serving)

Lunch & Dinner (each):

- Protein - 5-6 ounces (1-2 hand sizes)
- Veggies - Half a plate (extra if none at breakfast)
- Fat - 1-2 sources

Post-Dinner:

- Herbal tea
- Probiotic supplement or fermented food

Snacks (1-2/day, optional/as needed):

- Protein and/or Healthy fat as the base of each snack (see snack list)

Check the Food List and meal examples for foods to fit each of the above categories

How Much Do I Eat?

No weighing, counting calories or food measuring is needed. Simply choose 1-2 items from each category and eat until you are full, but not overly stuffed. Your plate should have a lot of green vegetables, about a third of space for protein, and a small amount of space for fat.

A rough estimate for each food group, includes:

- **Protein:** 1-2 palm sizes/deck of cards (4-8 oz)
- **Veggies:** Unlimited (about 1/2 your plate)
- **Fruit:** Handful/fist size, Bananas/Apples- ½ large or 1 small
- **Starch:** Fist size (1/3- ½ cup)
- **Fats:** 1-2 thumb size, golf-ball size, 1/2 avocado
- **Water:** 1/2 bodyweight in ounces

Master Fuel List
Variety is the spice of life! And, thankfully, there are hundreds of foods that fall into a "real food" nutrition template (i.e. you don't have to eat chicken and broccoli or dry salads).

Here's some inspiration for tons of foods, as well as meal ideas and a sample day of eating within a real-food body (and mind) balancing protocol.

Foods to Eat in Abundance:

Meat (Opt for organic, grass-fed, cage free meats as much as possible):

- Grass-fed Beef
- Grass-fed Bison
- Chicken
- Hen
- Lamb
- Turkey (Nitrate-free)

- Pasture-raised Whole Eggs (Chicken, goose, duck, quail)
- Sausage & Bacon/Turkey Bacon (Look for organic, nitrate-free versions)
- Deli meats (Nitrate-free; Applegate Farms is good brand sold most everywhere)
- Wild Game (Reindeer, Venison, Rabbit, Alligator, Emu, Elk, Kangaroo, Buffalo)
- Duck, Quail, Pheasant
- Organ meats (heart, liver, tongue)
- Pork (tenderloin, pork chops)

Plant-Based Proteins:

- Lentils
- Beans
- Quinoa
- Seeds and Nuts
- Nutritional Yeast
- Nuts
- Peas
- Seeds
- Spirulina

Seafood (Wild-caught sources are optimal):

- Fish, such as: Salmon, Tuna, Cod, Bass, Snapper, Mahi-Mahi, Mackerel, Arctic Char, Halibut, Walleye, Haddock, Herring, etc
- Shrimp
- Sardines
- Lobster
- Crab
- Oysters
- Mussels
- Clams
- Scallops
- Squid

Vegetables (Aim for 1-2 veggies with each meal and a variety of colors!):

Leafy Greens

- Chard
- Kale
- Lettuce
- Mustard
- Collards
- Parsley
- Spinach
- Beet greens
- Sweet potato leaves
- Arugula
- Baby greens
- Endive
- Romaine Lettuce
- Butterhead Lettuce
- Turnip Greens
- Cabbage

Other Fibrous Veggies

- Broccoli
- Asparagus
- Bean Sprouts
- Zucchini
- Yellow Squash
- Kale
- Brussels Sprouts
- Radicchio
- Cauliflower
- Bok Choy
- Artichoke
- Hearts of palm

- Cucumber
- Celery & Celery Root
- Bell peppers
- Mushrooms
- Bell Peppers
- Seaweed
- Sea Vegetables
- Onions
- Watercress
- Water Chestnut
- Radish
- Kohlrabi
- Okra
- Leeks
- Green Beans
- Onion
- Pickles
- Snow Peas
- Shallots
- Tomato, raw
- Garlic
- Capers
- Fennel
- Horseradish
- Parsley

Starchy Vegetables

- Sweet Potatoes (Jewel, Garnet, Jersey, Purple and Japanese)
- Yams
- Carrots
- Potatoes (Red, Yukon Gold, Purple, New, etc.)
- Butternut squash
- Spaghetti, delicata, or acorn squash
- Eggplant
- Beets and Beet Root

- Yucca
- Parsnip
- Plantain
- Cassava root
- Pumpkin
- Tapioca
- Arrowroot
- Rutabaga
- Turnip
- Jicama
- Taro
- Chayote

Fruit:

- Acai Berry
- Apple (1/2 medium-large apple)
- Apricot
- Bananas (1/2 medium/large=serving)
- Berries (blueberries, blackberries, boysenberries, cranberries, elderberry, goji, raspberry, strawberry)
- Cantaloupe
- Cherry
- Coconut
- Date
- Fig
- Grapes
- Grapefruit
- Guava
- Kiwi
- Mango
- Nectarine
- Oranges
- Lemon
- Lime
- Melons

- Papaya
- Peach
- Pear
- Persimmon
- Plums
- Pineapples
- Passion fruit
- Pomegranate
- Pumpkin
- Plum
- Raisin
- Tangerine
- Watermelon

Nuts/Seeds (Healthy fat!):

- Almonds
- Macadamia
- Walnuts
- Hazelnuts
- Pecans
- Cashews
- Chestnuts
- Brazil nuts
- Pistachio
- Tiger Nut
- Pine nuts
- Chia seeds
- Hemp Seeds
- Pistachios
- Pumpkin seeds
- Sesame seeds
- Sunflower seeds
- Flaxseed
- Natural nut butter/seed-butter (no salt/sugar added)

Oils or Fats (Make sure you are getting 1-2 healthy fats or nuts/
seeds with every main meal for optimal digestion and absorption of
nutrients):

- Pastured Egg Yolks
- Grass-fed meat
- Organic Bacon
- Wild-caught Fatty Fish (salmon, sardines, mackerel)
- Avocado (1 small, 1/3 – ½ large)
- Oils (Avocado, Coconut, Olive [Cold-Pressed, not cold-pro-
  cessed], Walnut, Macadamia nut, Sesame, Hemp, Pumpkin
  Seed, Red Palm Oil, etc)
- Coconut Milk, butter, and flakes (unsweetened)
- Grass-fed butter
- Ghee
- Duck fat
- Non-hydrogenated lard
- Beef Tallow
- Mayo (Avocado oil-based; avoid brands with canola oil or
  sugar)
- Palm Shortening (for baking)
- Olives

Legumes or Grains (Pre-soak before cooking, it prevents diffi-
cult-to-digest phytates/lectins found in grains from irritating your
stomach):

- Jasmine, Brown, Basmati, or White Rice
- Flaxseeds
- Steel-cut Oats (gluten-free)
- Quinoa
- Beans (black, kidney, white, fava, mung, etc.)
- Chickpeas
- Lentils
- Barley
- Buckwheat
- Spelt

- Sourdough
- Gluten-free bread (almond flour/coconut flour, cassava flour and tapioca flour sources are *preferred*, before something like Udi's or other mainstream gluten-free bread)

Dairy Foods (Full fat, raw, grass-fed organic sources are best)

- Grassfed butter
- Ghee
- Plain or Greek Yogurt with Live Active Cultures as the only ingredient
- Kefir (plain, Live Active Cultures)
- Whole grass-fed organic milk
- Organic, grass-fed full-fat Cottage cheese
- Fresh, raw cheese (cheddar, goat's cheese, fresh mozzarella)

Spices (Unlimited natural herbs and spices):

- Sea salt/Himalayan Sea Salt
- Black pepper
- Basil
- Cayenne Pepper
- Chili Powder
- Cilantro
- Cinnamon
- Cumin
- Oregano
- Parsley
- Rosemary
- Sage
- Thyme
- Turmeric
- Onion Powder
- Garlic
- Allspice
- Bay leaves
- Ginger

Gut Intuition: Digestive Wellness

How is *your* digestion?

Since your gut is the gateway to health, if you have a poorly functioning digestive system or "leaky gut," you can bet your bottom dollar that your intuitive eating cues will also be thrown off.

On top of eating real whole foods, a baseline gut-health protocol is a game-changer for reawakening your gut intuition and enhancing digestion.

Here are 8 simple daily practices that will help you reawaken your gut intuition via your gut itself, better than any pill, Tums, laxative or other quick-fix.

Baseline Love-Your-Gut Protocol

1. Take a Probiotic & Prebiotic Daily. Probiotics are supplements that contain healthy gut bacteria, necessary for maintaining a healthy bacterial balance in your gut—helping strengthen your immune system, enhance digestion and nutrient absorption, promote brain balance and balance blood sugar. In recent years, probiotics have gotten a lot of hype, but not all probiotics are created equal. Generally speaking, you get what you pay for. If probiotic strains are *not* listed on a label, this can be a sign of not be getting the right formula. Lastly, varying up your strains is essential.

Similar to your body's need for variety in foods, you want a blend or variety of different organisms, including soil-based or spore-based organisms and lactic-acid organisms (Most supplements *only* supply the lactic acid forms). Recommendations for the "best of all worlds" include taking soil or a spore-based formula like Prescript Assist, Megaspore Probiotic or Garden of Life Primal Defense Ultra, along with one to two servings of fermented foods daily.

2. Eat Fermented Foods & Prebiotic Foods. Incorporate kombucha, kimchi, kefir, sauerkraut, fermented veggies and fermented yogurt, along with prebiotic foods like cooked and cooled potatoes or sweet potatoes, Jasmine white rice, green-tipped bananas and plantains, onions, leeks asparagus and a supplemental form of probiotics (with "soil-based organisms" or "spore-forming organisms" over lactic acid bacteria formulas) and a pre-biotic fiber, like Partially Hydrolyzed Guar Gum. In addition, other gut-loving foods include: Coconut oil, coconut milk and other healthy fats, wild-caught fish (1-2 times per week) and pastured or grass-fed meats, dark leafy greens and veggies with every meal (especially cooked or steamed), ginger, garlic, turmeric and curcumin, pineapple, papaya, meat and bone broth and herbal teas.

3. Treat Your Body Like a Ferrari. On top of eating real food, food quality matters. You wouldn't put cheap gas in a Ferrari would you? Well, your body is a Ferrari and to ensure top quality goes into the tank, shop for quality sources, and be sure to cook and properly prepare your food as often as you can.

- Opt for organic, grass-fed, pasture-raised and wild-caught *real* foods (not necessarily "organic Oreos" or "organic Mac & Cheese")
- Eat in 17-18 home cooked meals every week (80%). Many restaurants cook their food in vegetable oils (hydrogenated oils, margarine) that clog up your gut and sneak sugars in unexpected places—like sauces and salad dressing.
- Soak nuts, grains and seeds in water before consumption
- Wash veggies and fruits thoroughly before consuming
- Food lasts about three days once prepared (in the fridge). Freeze leftovers if needed.

4. Recognize the Culprits. Aside from eating out, there could be everyday foods you are sensitive to, and that impact your digestion. Dairy, gluten, and sugar are commonly known gut irritants—but there may be other foods that may equally affect you, like FODMAPs for example— types of carbohydrates that are easily fermented by gut bacteria and subsequently produce gas and distension in some people.

FODMAPs is an acronym for:

- **F**ermentable
- **O**ligosaccharides (eg. Fructans and Galacto-oligosaccharides
- **D**isaccharides (eg. Lactose)
- **M**onosaccharides (eg. excess Fructose)
- and
- **P**olyols (eg. Sorbitol, Mannitol, Maltitol, Xylitol and Isomalt)

Some FODMAPS include: artichoke, beans, apples, avocado, cauliflower, cabbage, processed meats, cashews, pears, cherries, coconut, onions, and of course, artificial sugars. Other common intolerances some people have are nightshade fruits and vegetables, including: potatoes, tomatoes, eggplant, goji berries, and black pepper.

Other foods that may be gut-irritating include: Eggs, nuts, seeds, beans, large portions of meat and potatoes in one sitting, and fruit (eaten with other complex foods). No, not ALL of these foods will be a culprit for your body. Use your food journal to help you problem solve here. Get in touch with how foods make you *feel*.

5. Drink Water. Half your bodyweight in ounces per day of clean filtered water. It's a fact. Your body is made up of a lot of water, so of course water is what's going to help move things along. Get a stainless steel water bottle to keep on your A-game.

6. Chew Your Food. Digestion begins in your mouth. When you break your food down well first in your mouth, it will move through your digestive tract much easier. The same thing goes for *how you eat your food*—slow down. Chew, chew, swallow. Chew, chew, swallow. Optimal digestion happens in a *parasympathetic state*. Read: Relaxed. So set aside at least 20-30 minutes to eat your meal—and teach your kids this process. Put your fork down between bites. Rest and digest.

7. Boost Stomach Acid. Drink one tablespoon of apple cider vinegar mixed with 2-4 ounces of water before meals, or consider an HCL Supplement. One or two capsules with each protein-based meal (600-1200 mg) can help boost your stomach and distill GI distress if bloating, gas or loose stools are common for you. (Note: Do not take HCL if you are currently taking PPI's for heartburn or reflux). In addition, digestive enzymes can help break down your food post-meal.

8. Catch Some Zzzz's. Sleep is when our bodies restore—digestive processes included. Did you know when we are under-sleeping, constipation and bloating are more common? And while 8 hours sounds like the *ideal*...sometimes it's hard to make it happen! If you have been sleeping less than 7-9 hours most nights, begin by aiming to get at least 30-60 minutes more of sleep (whatever that means for you).

Finding Your 80/20 Balance

Once you've established a baseline for what "real food" and "digestive wellness" means, building these practices into your daily life will naturally begin to re-set your internal cues and palate.

Eating real food may not seem natural at first, particularly if you've trained your body, brain and tastebuds to subsist off of foods it was not designed to thrive upon.

I have been there, done that and got the t-shirt! Crystal Light, Diet Coke, Lean Cuisines, Slim Fast Shakes, Quest Bars, Light n' Fit yogurts, Splenda, Kashi Krunch, fat-free ice cream, sugar-free Jell-O, turkey sandwiches on whole wheat bread and pretzel sticks were my jam.

However, for the body to develop credible associations and cues around food — including feeling satiated, nourished and knowing what nutrients it truly needs (iron from dark leafy greens, amino acids from pastured-eggs, Vitamin B from grass-fed meats, Vitamin C from bright orange citrus)— it needs to be communicated with honestly. Otherwise, it can't learn!

In nature, animals can eat and know what their body needs—limiting their meal size not because they're stuffed and couldn't possibly eat another bite, but because they've hit a secondary compound wall (i.e. met their nutritional needs beyond counting calories).

When we eat processed, packaged, sugary (or artificially sweetened) and additive-filled foods, use food to cope with our emotions, or look more to diet rules (rather than listening to our own bodies), we actually turn off our brain's ability to signal "I'm nourished."

Instead, synthetic foods, emotional eating, or lack thereof, *illuminate receptors* our brain that make us addicted to wanting and craving bad foods, as well as cloud our thinking as to what true fullness, satiation, and nourishment looks like

Even if you eat real foods, but are basing what you eat more on food rules, food fears or rituals, rather than *listening to your body and your gut,* they may not be the right foods for you (or your digestion).

But what about chocolate, sugar cravings, birthday parties and eating out? Does intuitive eating mean never eating a treat or going out to eat again?!

Heck no!

This is where 80/20 balance comes into play, along with *reconnecting to your food.*

Remember, vacations happen. Eating out happens. Birthday parties happen. Non-organic spinach or chicken happens. Going to friends' dinner parties or hot dates happen. And guess what: It's ok! Food cannot hurt you.

Live by the 80/20 rule, not striving only for perfection. Eat in abundance, rather than restriction, asking yourself: "What **can** I eat?" As opposed to: "What **can't** I eat?" There are so many foods that fall into that 80% goodness, and when we build the majority of our meals upon real, whole foods, then the other 20% comes out in the wash.

Break Out: Connecting to Your Food: Beyond Meal Plans

In addition to keeping an 80/20 (balanced) perspective with food for optimal "intuition," eating to nourish your body with what it *wants* goes far beyond simply following a meal plan or program (even if it is real food). This is perhaps the reason why many people go on diets, even real food diets, only to completely do the opposite come Day 31, when they can have all-you-can-eat pizza, chocolate, carbs, etc.

An intuitive relationship with food isn't just about going through the motions of eating real food. It ALSO involves connecting with our food (beyond checking off boxes for proteins, fats and carbs). Here are eight considerations that influence how we *intuitively* connect to food beyond a meal plan:

1. Seasonal Eating
Not necessarily fruitcake at Christmas or turkey and dressing at Thanksgiving, but rather eating foods that are *in season*—foods at their peak of nutrition and abundance. Seasonal eating sounds obvious, but this is more than just buying what's in season and grown locally. It's also about **developing a cooking mindset that compliments seasonal patterns and how your body *feels* during these seasons.**

If you think about how our ancestors or even great-great-grandparents ate (before the processed food generation), they ate what was available on the land at different times of year and geographically. For instance, during the winter, heartier foods like potatoes, squashes, nuts, and meats provided robust sustenance for warmth. During the summer months, lighter, colorful fresh foods—fresh salads, fruits, crisp vegetables— provided energy without weighing them down. They weren't able to go to the grocery store and buy just anything. Seasonal eating provided them with what their bodies intuitively needed.

Here's are some seasonal feelings and foods:

- **Spring Feelings:** Renewed Energy, New Beginning, Rapid Start
  Eat: Young sweet, pungent foods (beets, carrots, greens, sprouts, honeydew melon, green beans, asparagus) and herbs (basil, fen

- **Summer Feelings:** Joy, Brightness, Light, Creativity, Engagement
  Eat-Brightly colored fruits and veggies (salads, cucumber, sprouts, melons, apricots, yams, beans, peas, summer squashes, tomatoes, berries, broccoli, cauliflower, eggplant, peaches, watermelon, Lima beans) and herbs (mint, chamomile, basil, cilantro). Heavy foods on hot days may cause sluggishness (meats, eggs, excess nuts and seeds), so minimize heat in your cooking.

- **Fall Feelings:** Harvest & Gathering, Storing up fuel, Recollecting Scattered Energy
  Eat: Sour foods (sauerkraut, olives, sourdough) and moist Autumn foods (spinach, pear, apple, persimmon).

- **Winter Feelings:** Grounding, Storage, Warmth, Heartiness
  Eat: Warm hearty soups and stews, hearty veggies (dark leafy greens, potatoes, sweet potatoes, winter squash, carrots, onions, garlic, pumpkins, Brussels sprouts), citrus, (pineapple and grapes), nuts, bitter foods (watercress, endive, quinoa), salty foods (miso, seaweed), pastured and grass-fed meats, and warming spices (cloves, cinnamon, cumin, cayenne, turmeric, fenugreek, ginger, fennel). Slow-cooked and braised foods are great in the winter.

Note: This is not an exhaustive list of foods, nor does it mean if you don't see a food on the list, that you *can't* have it during that time of year. More than anything, tune in to seasonal eating to get the most out of foods in touch with your body's rhythms during that season. For more info on what's in season in your area, check out: **http://www. sustainabletable.org/seasonalfoodguide/** and also pay attention to sales in your local grocery store. Typically produce that's on sale (and fresh looking) is most in-season.

2. Culture
Cultural intuition is unique to your own cultural background or area of the world in which you live (or visit). Japan or China? Rice, fish, meat (chicken, pork or beef) and vegetables will more than likely be part of the meal, along with ginger, onion and soy sauce seasonings. Greece? Greek dishes like Tzatziki, souvlaki, gyros, dolmas, and falafel are musts, along with plenty of olive oil, olives, vegetables and fresh meats. Spain? Tapas, paella, gazpacho, Spanish omelettes, Chorizo, seafood and shellfish, olive oil, and vegetables are on the menu. India? Curries, stews, lentils, flatbreads, yogurt, chickpeas, and goat's milk are some of the top picks.

Think about how your own cultural background influences your intuition—even the culture in your own home. Did you grow up eating meat and potatoes, spicy foods, takeout, ethnic foods? How has your own culture influenced your food choices and what sounds or feels good?

3. Experiences & Environments
Our varied experiences and environments at different times and seasons of life can also influence what we eat—and want to eat—within that context. During college, for instance, the experience of being on-the-go, living in a dorm and being low on cash, meant you lived off of Ramen, free pizza, salad bars and cafeteria food, and you viewed the weekends when mom and dad visited to treat you to a fancy steak dinner that you savored.

Or, every year on summer vacation, you "fall off the bandwagon" or eat things you otherwise don't typically eat once you're in vacation mode—intuitively you've longed to "be free" from your usual routine. Come January, at the turn of the new year, maybe you experience a desire to reset your body and your mindset. The experience of fresh beginnings and the societal environment around you (ads marketed towards healthy eating and fitness) inspires a fresh pep in your step to "crave" more salads, fresh fruits and home-cooked meals.

What current experiences or environments shape your intuition?

4. Social Eating

Peer pressure and "groupthink" goes far beyond high school. A study on the eating habits of medical students found that the majority of students ate balanced meals, veggies and fruits "regularly," and had a low consumption of fried foods simply because they were more aware of healthy living and choices, and were amongst like-minded people who equally thought about leading a healthy lifestyle.

Other studies have shown that societal norms (what others eat around us) and models of food behavior influence our own food choices. Around friends who are eating popcorn, soda and sour straws at the movies? Chances are you will want a bag of popcorn—or at least something to eat alongside them. All the cool kids bring a Lunchable to school? Then your PB & J looks like chopped liver to you. Everyone at work brings their lunch, or eat out? Depending on what the group does, you may do the same.

Conforming to a group norm is a rewarding experience, and eating with others further amplifies the experience. Additionally, positive social feedback from peers increases our own expected liking and positive attitudes towards certain foods, as well as the internal valuation of those foods. Think about your own social situations and how they impact your food desires, cravings, and ability to eat intuitively.

5. Cooking

The art of cooking is an adventure in intuitive eating all its own. Have you ever asked the question: "What sounds good for dinner?" Your nose, your tastebuds and your own experience (and confidence) in the kitchen may determine that answer. The cool thing? Even if you don't feel completely confident in your Masterchef abilities right now, there's no time like the present to experiment and connect with a new skill of intuitive eating. And, in the words of master-cook Julia Child, "You don't have to cook fancy or complicated masterpieces - just good food from fresh ingredients."

Recipes aside, home-prepared meals foster a different sort of relationship with food, wherein you become more mindful to the pairings, seasonings, spices, herbs, variety, freshness and presentation of the food before you. Whether you whip up a one-pan hash with ground meat, greens, sweet potatoes, cinnamon and sea salt, create a new spaghetti squash casserole you were inspired to create from Pinterest, or blend a colorful smoothie, cooking and preparing foods forces you think: *What really sounds good to eat?*

6. Fun
Food is a symbol of "fun" for different occasions and meals. Intuitively, we may not want another dry chicken breast and broccoli—and that's okay. Curry, cinnamon, red-pepper flakes or simply another meat and veggie actually sound better. Other ways we may seek "fun" with food and the eating experience include: Trying a new restaurant, getting crafty with the presentation (like ants on a log), baking holiday cookies or classic casseroles you only eat once per year, or celebrating special occasions. How does a desire for fun impact your food cues?

7. Cravings
Cravings often get a bad rep, but not all cravings are "bad" or emotionally driven. Cravings are your body's way of communicating with you, "Hey, I need something." For instance, when you crave sugar, your body may actually need energy, and since sugar is a quick source of energy, it's what your body may have been trained to ask for (especially if you frequently eat it).

The same can be said when you begin basing your diet on more real foods. You can retrain your body to actually crave and signal to you the real foods it's been wanting all along—be it glucose from sweet potatoes, healthy fat and linoleic acid from grass-fed butter, Omega-3's from salmon or halibut, or magnesium and Vitamin K from dark leafy greens.

8. How Do You Feel?

It's a question we will come back to time and time again. Brussels sprouts may be healthy, but if you get gas and bloating every time you eat them, then intuitively, they probably won't feel as good when eating them. Or, some real-food protocols may say "rice is bad for you," but perhaps, for your body, you feel good when you incorporate some rice into your diet. Queso and chips may sound good intuitively, but after eating them, you have second thoughts as you find yourself in the bathroom with loose stools.

Every BODY is different, and by getting to know your body and what genuinely works best (or doesn't work) within the context of real whole foods most of the time, you will learn a powerful new language: Listening.

Break Out: Food Intolerances vs. Food Fears: What's the Difference?

As you begin to incorporate more real foods into your diet and become more aware of how food makes you feel, it can be easy to fall into a conundrum of questions about your body's ability to tolerate (or not tolerate) certain foods you may, at one time, have not thought twice about.

Knowledge is power, but for some, unnecessary food fears or food rules can evolve and it's important to recognize the differences in food fears and food intolerances (to help you keep sane).

How do you know the difference in a food intolerance or allergy vs. a food fear or a food aversion? Well…ask yourself "How do I **feel** when I eat this certain food—physically **and** mentally?"

There is a difference!

Common Signs of Food Intolerances & Allergies

- Bloated or gassy shortly after eating
- Constipation
- Low energy
- Skin breakouts
- Anemia
- Low immunity
- Allergies
- Hormonal imbalances
- Anxiety
- Lowered mood
- Insatiable cravings for foods that make you feel bloated or gassy
- Heart palpitations or racing heart
- Achy joints
- Sneezing & coughing
- Headaches & lightheadedness
- Gastric distress, diarrhea, or nausea
- Foggy eyes & brain

Common Signs of Food Fear

- Overthinking food
- Making yourself believe and think food is hurting you
- Correlating eating with weight gain
- Counting the calories in the food and worrying about eating too many
- Avoidance of foods or food groups without ever having tasted or tried them before

- Avoidance of social gatherings around food
- Basing food choices off of self-imposed rules
- Giving yourself a stomachache over the stress around food
- Pre-planning your foods and calories
- Having to "earn" your food

Sometimes lines blur. A missing link many people fail to recognize is knowing when they have or haven't eaten "right" based on how they *feel*—more so than what any rule in a diet book says or achievement you feel by not eating certain foods.

On the contrary, a missing link on the path to food freedom and intuitive eating **is recognition of what food intolerances** really look like. While food freedom is amazing, a general respect for your body's ability to digest (or not digest) certain foods are also necessary.

Food Intolerance & Allergies 101

It's important to recognize what food intolerances and allergies are. The two are often thought to be *similar,* but there are several distinct differences.

A true **food allergy** is an immune system response.

It is caused when the body mistakes an ingredient in food — usually a protein — as harmful and creates a defense system (antibodies) to fight it. An **allergic reaction** occurs when the antibodies are battling an "invading" food protein, such as: Rash or hives, nausea, stomach pains, diarrhea, itchy skin, chest pains, shortness of breath, or lung swelling. The most common food allergies are shellfish, nuts, fish, eggs, peanuts, and milk.

A **food intolerance** is a digestive system response rather than an immune system response.

It occurs when something in a food irritates a person's digestive system or when a person is unable to properly digest, or break down, the food. In other words, you eat a food your body doesn't know how to handle and your body goes "May day! I don't know what to do with this!" It may present in the signs and symptoms mentioned above, though usually less severe.

Food intolerances vary more considerably than food allergies, though common sensitivities include: lactose, found in milk and other dairy products, gluten, grains, nuts and seeds, FODMAPs (onions, garlic, apples, bananas, avocado, tomatoes), nightshades (potatoes, peppers), and of course, packaged and processed foods. Not necessarily ALL of them, but some of them.

Diagnosis

Both food allergy and food intolerance tests can be diagnosed via **lab testing**, as well as **mindful eating, elimination testing** and **the Cocoa's Pulse Test**.

Lab Testing

For clinical lab testing, Cyrex Labs provides one of the most robust food allergy and intolerance testing, as it looks for all sorts of proteins individuals may be allergic or intolerant to—not just the "basics."

For instance, a lot of GI doctors know how to screen for celiac disease, they'll typically test for antibodies to gluten only. If some of these tests are positive, then they may perform a biopsy to determine if enteropathy or tissue damage is present, but if the tests are negative, the patient is usually told that they don't have celiac or gluten intolerance—end of the story. However, research shows that people can and do react to several other components in wheat above and beyond alpha-gliadin, which is why a robust food allergy and intolerance panel can be beneficial for the full picture.

Mindful Eating

Getting in touch with how food makes you feel can also get you far. Many of us are simply disconnected from the correlation between food and feelings.

For example, as a kid growing up, I was not a picky eater. I ate whatever my mom served me or packed in my lunch for school, and simply saw food as something necessary to get me from basketball practice to dance class to using brain power for my long division math problems. Food also tasted good, and my go-to foods were all based on what my tastebuds told me they liked (i.e. sugar!): Pop-tarts. Eggo Waffles. Macaroni and cheese. Spaghetti-O's. Fruit Rollups and Gushers. Wheat Thins Crackers and Kraft Singles cheese slices. Chocolate milk.

As a kid of the 'processed' food generation, grains, dairy and sugar made up the bulk of my childhood diet. Fast forward to my later teen and college years: More aware of how particular foods impacted the body (in my teen mind: made you 'fat' or 'skinny'), I developed a diet mentality, and the bulk of my nutrition consisted of: Crystal Light and Diet Sodas, Lean Cuisine frozen meals, low-fat grains and dairy products, canned protein drinks, egg whites, and oats flavored with Splenda packets.

While both of these seasons of my life (childhood and early 20s) reflect two completely different food philosophies (processed foods and diet foods), one thing was the same: my symptoms:

- Fluctuating constipation, bloating and loose stools
- Frequent nausea or gastric discomfort
- Sluggish digestion post-meals
- Frequent gas
- Spikes in energy, followed soon by lows in energy
- Poor mental focus

These were my norm.

It was not until giving a real-food nutrition template a chance (cutting out the grains, the dairy, the artificial sweeteners, the sugar, the low fat intake) that I had **my LIGHTBULB moment**: *Food actually impacts how I FEEL!*

It's not just about the taste or what you've been told foods will do for you (ex. "You must drink this pre-workout powder," or, "Nuts are heart healthy," or "Avoid sugar by using artificial sweeteners", etc.).

The same thing happened on a "real foods" diet, during a brief stint when I resolved I needed to "go paleo" and later, "go Keto." This entailed ZERO non-paleo foods, very low carbs and low sugar (including fruit), and guilt if I entertained the thought of anything outside my righteous way of eating. Until one day, I ate half a banana and a sweet potato—in the same day—and I realized, the world continued to turn. Another day I tried sushi—with rice, and one more day, protein powder with a little bit of stevia in it, and I really realized that life went on. Food DOES impact how you feel, and instead of listening too the food rules and guidelines you've imposed upon yourself, what would it be like to experiment with a variety of foods and determine for yourself how food makes you feel?

Elimination Testing

If you suspect a food intolerance, the easiest way to test yourself is to simply try eliminating the trigger food from your diet altogether—for several days. At least 3 to 7 days. Note how you feel. Better? Symptom free? No change? After your time is up, reintroduce it with a meal and…just see. How do you feel now? Did any symptoms return?

If that's not it, then it may be something else like a different trigger food, the quality of the food (organic vs. non organic), a lack of digestive health and support, stress—or any combination of these.

Note: For most accurate results with the food elimination test, consider testing one food—as opposed to multiple foods—at a time. Or,

if you do cut out more than one food, it will work best if you reintroduce foods one at a time.

Coca Pulse Test
The Coca Pulse Test is a nutritional therapy evaluation that helps determine any "allergic tension" an individual may have. Here's how to do it.

- Collect any foods you'd like to test for possible food allergies
  (ex. oatmeal, bread, nuts, cheese, rice, tomato, apples, eggs,
  etc.).
- Take your resting pulse x 1 minute while seated and relaxed.
- Then place the test food in your mouth.
- Salivate it for 30 seconds.
- Retake your resting pulse x 1 minute while seated and relaxed.

If your pulse change by six beats or more, it is indicative of "allergic
tension." You can perform this for as many suspected foods as you
like.

Now the question turns to you: Are there particular foods you eat
that your body simply doesn't agree with?

How do you really know how or if certain foods are impacting you in
a negative way—particularly if you've been eating these foods, day in
and day out for 15-30 years? Or following food rules that seem good,
in theory (like eating sugar-free additives, or nuts for every snack)?

Are there certain foods you say you are "intolerant" to, but really just
fear?

You actually may not even realize how these foods are making you feel
until you dig in and examine it further.

And if you are "intolerant" it may not actually be the food itself you
are intolerant to, but rather you *may have* a case of **poor gut health
or leaky gut** directly impacting your digestion and ability to tolerate

foods. Check in with yourself and really consider how you're feeling when eating different foods.

Break Out: 'Good' & 'Bad' Foods Don't Exist

Along the same lines of pushing your food fears aside, a popular saying within the intuitive eating world is: "There's no such thing as 'good' and 'bad' foods."

But is it true? After all, we *know a* McDonald's cheeseburger and French fries has a completely different nutrient profile than a chicken breast and sweet potato.

Is there **really** such things as "no good or bad foods" or "everything in moderation" (when the truth seems so obvious)?

Yes and no. Allow me to explain…

Determining Whether Food is "Good" or "Bad"

For years, I was in and out of eating disorder treatment and I was told that, to be "normal," I had to eat pizza on Friday nights, birthday cake on my birthday and Egg McMuffins for breakfast. Salads were frowned upon at dinner outings, and if I wanted an apple or almonds for a snack, the staff scoffed at me for choosing the "safe" option.

On the contrary, watch any diet commercial, read news headlines or pick up any best-selling book in the health section at Barnes & Noble, and you'll surely find prescriptions and protocols to "Cut sugar," "Choose whole wheat over white," and "Eat less processed foods."

In one definition (like eating disorder recovery), a "healthy relationship with food" means eating Egg McMuffins. In another, a "healthy relationship with food" means NOT eating Egg McMuffins.

The truth?

The real answer to the "Is there good and bad foods?" question is...
You get to decide. It's not a distinctive "yes," or a "no." Instead it
is 100% customized to you—depending on your heart, head, experiences, and personal health status. The views, attitudes and relationships we have with our bodies, our food and ourselves are far more
important than the nutrition labels, or stereotypes, of any food we put
into our body.

Example: An Egg McMuffin is not "good" for me, especially if I eat
a lot of processed foods regularly, on the regular, want to improve
my gut health, or if I am looking for the most optimal, energizing
nourishment.

However, an Egg McMuffin may very well be "good" for me, if it
symbolizes something far greater than the actual nutrients going into
my body. While consuming them daily is not recommended, eating
an Egg McMuffin—and living to tell about it—was one of the most
mind-freeing exercises I could have done for myself because it allowed
me to:

- Recognize that what doesn't kill me, makes me stronger
- Go on vacations and participate in food experiences and go
  with the flow ("Hey I lived to talk about that Egg McMuffin!")
- Gave me an appreciation (and passion) to discover more about
  the role of food in actually nourishing my body. Eating Egg
  McMuffins every Friday morning for a year inspired me to
  explore and integrate "food as medicine," and for the first
  time, embrace real, whole fresh foods as life-giving nutrition to
  my body (mind and soul).

See the difference?

Yes. Certain foods do have more nutrients than others.

Yes. There is no denying that real food like animal proteins, vegetables, fruits and healthy fats (like avocados, coconut oil, olive oil, fatty fish and nuts/seeds) are foods your body recognizes and thrives upon, much like a plant thrives upon water and sunshine.

And yes, the Standard American Diet is laden with sugars, processed foods and refined grains that do contribute to disease and inflammation.

BUT…when I label foods as "good" or "bad," I give the food items a greater life and control of their own and set myself up for the diet mentality.

Eat in Abundance

This is the methodology I practice which helps bring clarity to the dilemma at hand.

Eating in abundance = Eating as "least restrictively as possible."

When you begin the art of intuitive eating and truly listening to your own body, you begin to recognize how certain foods truly make you feel/don't feel and what foods are good for your own gut health, mind health and energy.

"Eating in abundance" means maintaining an "**abundant**" mindset. Asking "what **can** I eat?" Instead of a restrictive mindset: "What do I have to eliminate? What CAN'T I have? What SHOULDN'T I have?"

Instead of saying, "I CAN'T have that," or "That's BAD for me," what would it be like to say things such as "What CAN I have?" and "What do I want?"

Eating in abundance also means instead of looking to rules and Google articles on whether food is good or bad for us, we simply turn inward. We ask ourselves: "How does this food make me feel?" and "How am I nourishing my body?"

The answer may very well become clearer.

You may happily eat brown rice, even though the latest research says that white rice is better.

Or you may find you do better when you eat some starch with your breakfast, whereas your friend swears by Intermittent Fasting or ketogenic Bulletproof coffee.

You must find what works for you specifically.

The Bottom Line
"Good" and "bad" foods don't exist.

More nutrient-dense foods exist. Less nutrient-dense and nourishing foods exist. And "good" and "bad" mentalities exist.

Aim to eat more nutrient-dense foods in abundance. Tune in to how certain foods do and don't nourish your body (how you feel, breakouts, gut health, etc.). Go on strike from unnecessary rules. Embrace opportunities to challenge old diet mentalities. And realize there is NO such thing as "perfection" or "perfect eating."

Lifestyle Factors & Intuition: Movement, Rest & Stress Busting

Last, but not least, before I give you the simple action steps to Redefine EVERYTHING you've learned up to now,I want to talk about three other essentials that affect how you feel physically : **Movement (i.e. fitness), Rest (sleep) and Stress Busting.**

Consider these three things the "cherry on top" to real food, gut love and an 80/20 balanced mindset for your intuition.

Movement

Do you have an exercise "drill sergeant?" A force in the back of your mind pushing you to do things with your body you don't always want to do? Or who tells you that you "suck" or that exercise is such a chore? A drag?

I did.

My drill sergeant often sounded like this: "Drop & give me 100!"

As soon as my alarm went off at 4:45 a.m., I could not do anything else until I had completed my 10-minute morning ab routine (fearing that my abs would turn to mush if I didn't stick to this religiously). It didn't stop there. Next I was off to the gym, where that little voice in the back of my head whipped me into shape—pushing me to suck it up on the StairMaster at level 20 for 45 minutes, then complete my hour-long weight routine, some HIIT sprints on the treadmill, and finish it off with another "easy" 45-minutes at level 15 this time.

A few hours passed. Then…it was back to the gym for round two. An hour in the gym between classes then back to afternoon class sessions, before hitting the gym for my last session of the day—another 2 to 3 hours, similar to my morning routine.

Rest for 4-5 hours. Repeat the next day. Then the next day.

Although my experience sounds extreme, any time we FORCE our bodies to do things that are not in our own best interest (or self-sabotage ourselves from doing things in our best interest), we run further from health (not closer to it).

Although I *thought* I was working out like that to "be healthy," I was actually doing the furthest thing from health.

Sometimes we also fall into the trap of just "checking off" our work-out list, instead of asking our bodies and ourselves: *How do you want to move today?*

Chances are, if you're like most fitness enthusiasts, you checked off your box or earned your gold star for getting in your gym time. Run? Swim? Spin class?

Check. Check. Check. Exercise complete...until the next day, when you have to **do the same thing again** (and if you don't, you may experience guilt or watch what you eat more closely).

Perhaps you're at the opposite end of the spectrum. If fitness is "not your thing," you often do everything else, BUT move your body:

- You watch Netflix
- Go to Happy Hour
- *Think* about going to the gym
- Cook a healthy dinner
- Or tell yourself, "tomorrow I'll do something"

Exercise is such a *chore.*

Whichever mentality or end of the spectrum you fall into, whenever we make exercise a formality, gold star we earn, or checklist in our heads rather than an expression of using our God-given limbs that move, heart that beats, endorphins that come alive and lungs that breathe, we get further away from *being human—movement.*

Movement vs. Exercise

Your body doesn't see exercise the same way you and I see it. We often see it as a checklist item. But, your body sees **exercise as _movement_.**

We often view exercise as a routine, dedicated time to sweat. Your body places no labels on it.

We see exercise as a specific structured time when we...

- Gather with others in a small room and jump up and down (bootcamp, pump class)
- Follow our FitBit's calculation of 3 miles exactly (a run)
- Move our legs fast to the beats of Beyonce on the spin bike (spin)
- Or press a bar up and down 10 times as fast as we can, in between box jumps and burpees, within an 8-minute time frame (CrossFit)

...then log calories burned, drink a protein shake, eat a big dinner (which we earned) or feel relieved to be "finished."

Your body doesn't see movement as formal exercise. **All your body sees is that it is *movement* time—and for as long as you're moving, it's working for you.**

Optimally, your body prefers *intuitive movement* if you *will* allow it:

- Sometimes it can (and wants to) pick up a heavy barbell 10-30 times.
- Other times, it has the power to run the length of a football field, walk back, then go again—fast.
- Other times, a long run or long hike sounds really good—getting lost and clearing your head, meditation and prayer.
- Sometimes, it's tight—and all it wants is a mobility session with a lacrosse ball and some low-intensity movement on a rower or incline walk.
- And other times, it likes to connect with a community or group workout, spurring your competitiveness to come out—and getting excited: it's ready to perform and...move.

As you raise awareness of your *old* beliefs and intuitions around exercise (either dreading it, or making yourself do it), here's are three new questions to ask yourself:

Reflection & Rule Break Project:

1. **What could "intuitive exercise"** —movement—**look like for you?** (No formalities, checklists, or "must-do-cardio to burn off that ice cream" needed).
2. **Why do you train?** Why do you do the particular exercises you do. List as many reasons as you can think of—and elaborate on them if you need.
3. **How can you buck the system today?** As hard as it may be to just say "NO!" to that exercise drill sergeant, do it. Do SOMETHING DIFFERENT than you usually do, whether it is a class, a new weight training program, a buddy workout, swimming, yoga, anything. Or get up and simply move, any way you want, if you've been holding off on exercise or movement, just get going.

Chances are, this type of movement *will look different every day.*

Intuitive Movement: In Practice

Movement and *fitness* are meant to enliven you and your body—not drain you, be a chore or be something you "have to do." Simply move how you were designed to move in a variety of ways and have some fun along the way.

I call this **Primal Movement**. In total, there are seven key primal movement patterns the human body was wired and created to do (without even thinking about it) to survive and thrive in our world, performing daily tasks and demands. Throughout the week, you'll see these moments trickle into your routine.

These include:

- Squatting
- Bending
- Lunging
- Pushing
- Twisting
- Pulling
- Walking, Jogging, Sprinting (Gait)

Also, Primal Movement means varying up types of movement: Strength, HIIT & Power, Aerobic Work, Flexibility, Walking, Active Rest and Rest.

Just like some days you eat chicken, other days you eat beef, or some days you eat broccoli and other days you eat squash, *variety* gives your body the "movement nutrition" it needs to thrive. Despite the dogma that you *need* to run 6 miles every day, workout 3-6 hours everyday, perform the same leg training routine on Mondays and upper body routine on Wednesdays, that CrossFit WODs are the only way to get a good workout in, or that lifting heavy things isn't good for your body because it will make you bulky. Stop overthinking it, and start loving your body through ***movement of all sorts***—walks, runs, classes, camps, spins, swims, jumping up and down, hikes, stretches, and everything in between. Instead of exercising try just moving.

What does this look like in practice?

Here's a sample of what Primal Movement (and variety) could look like in a given week to experience the best of *all* worlds of fitness:

Intuitive Movement Example:

- **Movement Monday:** Strength Day. A combo of weighted and bodyweight movements to get the blood flowing for the week.

- **Tabata/HIIT Tuesday:** Heart-pumping fun: sprints, Cross-Fit, bootcamp, and work-rest intervals.

- **Work It Wednesday:** Strength Day. Full-body strength work that will not leave you wishing you had run on the treadmill.

- **Thriving Thursday:** Active Rest Day. Movement, Yoga, something active but not intense, rejuvenating, low intensity aerobic work, maybe a long walk.

- **Fitness Friday:** Hybrid Day. Strength + Conditioning. A base of strength movements, coupled with some power and aerobic movements. Bootcamp. A workout video. Weights and a little bit of cardio. Your own thing in the gym.

- **Sweaty Saturday:** Break a sweat and get out of your routine. Do something new, different or out-of-the-norm. Keep it fun! Try a hip-hop class, warmed yoga flow, spin and weights, go on a run or hike with a friend, play sand volleyball or soccer, rent a kayak—the sky is the limit.

- **Slow Down Sunday:** Rejuvenate. Meal Prep, Walk, Yoga, do something outside, a Therapeutic Movement Session (bodyweight, low intensity movement), anything to rest, relax, and rejuvenate for the following week.

This comes out to be:

- 3-days of strength-based sessions
- 1-2 HIIT or class sessions
- And 1-3 days of walking, flexibility, yoga, active play or complete rest

Nitty Gritty Truths

Easier said than done? Still find it tough to be intuitive with movement and just move? Here are a few common questions and topics on many women's minds when it comes to the gym (and truth to set you free).

"But won't I get bulky?"

"I am scared of getting bulky," #SayMostWomen. "Bulking up" is one of the top-rated fears amongst women when it comes to the choice between Cardio or Weights. Obviously, running, Barre and pilates equal "long and lean" and strength training equal "bulk" right?

Many women back this common fear with claims like:

- "I have a slow metabolism."
- "Weight lifting makes me pack on muscle."
- "I am a heavier build."

It is true—just like snowflakes come in all shapes and sizes, there are all sorts of different body types. However, if you think picking up a dumbbell or looking at a donut is enough to make you "bulk up," think again. It's not going to happen.

Simply put, if you're a woman, you just don't have the hormonal support, especially regarding testosterone, to get bulky. Many women correlate strength training with the pictures of a sport associated with weights—like Bodybuilding or CrossFit women. Women who are athletes, training for that sport in mind and eating accordingly (or doing something else, like take supplements) to get muscle mass to be that way. They are the 1% of the population, born with the right genetics, to be doing that sport. There's no way the average woman can look that way by lifting weights as a part of her routine.

So how does a woman "get bulky?" A few reasons, including: Not eating enough (i.e. under-eating slows down our metabolism), doing only cardio, sleeping less than six hours most nights, avoiding fats and eating artificially sweetened diet foods, not listening to their body's intuitive eating cues, and maintaining unrealistic expectations.

"Don't I need to do a ton of crunches to get a six pack?"

No matter how many crunches you do, you *can't* spot-train your core (or any other body part for that matter). As much as you'd like to crunch until a six pack pops out, crunches and sit-ups alone are going to be a long road. The best exercises include anything that engages the total body and core—full body movements, like deadlifts, squats (especially front squats), front rack or back rack lunges, step-ups, toes-to-bar, GHD sit-ups and hyper extensions, strict presses, barbell rows, and bench presses.

Working these bigger muscle groups (as opposed to isolated crunch exercises) hits your full body and core for development. In addition, one of the greatest forms of exercise you can do for your overall health, body fat, and stress is walk—our bodies were primal-wired to walk in our day-to-day lives. As unsexy as walking may sound for abs or under-arm development, it's the simple things in life that make a big difference. Grab a friend to meet up with after work, take a stroll on your lunch break, park further from the door, maybe go on a nice hike during the weekend.

"Don't I need to do lots of cardio to lose weight or get fit?"

Less is more when it comes to working out. This can seem counter-intuitive in a culture where we are told "Calories in=Calories out." But seriously.

When we run like hamsters on wheels (working out all the time), similar to when we eat *fewer* calories (not more), our body goes into "reserve mode." It fights to hold on to what it's got—reducing overall energy expenditure and metabolism, even when you're off the treadmill or out of your fitness class. When it comes to your fitness, **the "Goldilocks approach" is best (just right).**

Also, here are a few other things too much working out—especially "chronic cardio"—does for your body:

> **You Don't Shed Body Fat.** The "move more" and "go long" philosophies *seem* to make sense, but your body can physiologically only go "so hard" for so long. The longer you train, the more "steady state" the workout becomes and the less burn you actually get. Exercise raises cortisol (i.e. stress). When our

bodies are stressed, they hold onto things (like body fat) as a reserve to continue to fight against stress.

You Decrease Your Lean Muscle & Tone. Muscle and "tone" grows and repairs in between workouts—not during them. So when we run and run or push the "more time=better" button every single day, we break our bodies down rather than building them up.

Your Digestion & Appetite Gets Thrown Off. Digestion occurs in a parasympathetic state (rest and digest). Workouts and active lifestyles are awesome, but when we do too much, a couple of things happen: 1) Stomach Acid production gets suppressed (we need stomach acid to break down our food) and 2) Body energy is devoted to muscle breakdown and repair—as opposed to digestive flow (so things slow down).

Intensity Goes Down. Like way down. You have three different energy systems to tap into when you workout: Aerobic (Endurance), Glycolytic (Power), and Anaerobic ATP (Strength). For all-around fitness, a blend of all three is ideal. Too much in any one zone and intensity will go down, naturally—but, particularly in that aerobic (endurance) zone (the longer steady state type exercise), the body can only last so long.

Your Hormones Get Out of Whack. We mentioned this some, but as noted in point 3, exercise induces a cortisol response, which is not a bad thing in moderation. However, when cortisol stays elevated, other hormones get out of balance. Like a seesaw, cortisol goes up, estrogen and testosterone go down, and vice versa.

You Get Disconnected from Your Body. You stop listening (or knowing how to listen) to your body.

"Won't I lose all my gains if I don't workout?"

First things first. Let's understand what regular exercise training can **DO** for your body. When you workout you:

- Boost endorphins and mood
- Get your blood flowing
- Break down muscle then build it back up
- Enhance your endurance and energy
- Boost your confidence
- Get better quality sleep
- Boost metabolic function

All this, you know. However, what happens when you workout *too* much? "Overtraining" is typically associated with:

- Poor digestion (constipation, bloating, leaky gut, low stomach acid)
- Breaking down muscle—which stays broken down
- Adrenal stress
- Thyroid imbalances
- Hyperactive immune system (inflammation and susceptibility to disease)
- Hormonal imbalances and decreased metabolic function
- Losing your period
- Spinning your wheels in the gym—with little to know results (plateaus)
- Mood imbalances and getting irritated more easily
- Increased preoccupation with food, fitness, and your body
- Becoming more critical of yourself
- Difficulty recovering and more easily fatigued

In short: No bueno (no good)!

The Real Truth: What Happens When You Don't Workout
So, we know what happens when you **do** workout, and we also know what happens when you workout **too much**.

But what happens when you don't workout on occasion? What happens when you skip a day at the gym? Take a week off for vacation? Just decide you'd rather go for a walk, or do yoga one day?

The answer: **Nothing**.

Nothing really happens. (At least nothing *negative).*

In fact, no study has proven that a rest day or rest period from exercise is harmful to your health or results. A review of 10 publications between 1988 and 2007 revealed that every available experiment concluded basically the same thing: "Across the board, low frequency training got the same or at least surprisingly good results as higher frequency." For instance, a comparison of one longer strength session per week, compared to 3 shorter sessions over the course of a week, showed both produced adequate strength gains in participants. Another study comparing 2 to 3 days per week of training found no difference in strength improvement.

Not to mention, when we take some time off, or become *less rigid* with our routine, our body may even thank us. Movement and exercise is a lifestyle, not a check-list, and when we view workouts and exercise as part of our lifestyle, we recognize that some days we may move more. Some days we may move less. Just like some nights you sleep 8 hours, others 6, and some days you have more of an appetite, and others less. Some days you move more, others less, and, at the end of the day, it all comes out in the wash.

Break Out: Finding Your Happy Weight

When was the first time you remember thinking (or caring) about a number?

We live in a world obsessed with the number on a scale. Almost half of American children between 1st and 3rd grade want to be thinner and half of 9 and 10 year old girls are dieting.

Unfortunately, many in our society correlate weight loss and that number with "health."

Here's a challenge for you: Simply observe and reflect upon the "health" messages you see and hear in a given day.

A look at magazine covers scream claims like: "Lose 5 pounds in 5 days," infomercials for a fitness video tempt potential customers with phrases like, "tighten and tone," trainers in gyms sell the secret to what every human "wants" - weight loss. Emails in your inbox boast insider tips for boosting your metabolism and chiseling your waist, and the labels on many different food products in the grocery store remind us they are "zero calorie" and "sugar free"—closely tied to this value of weighing *less*.

But does the *goal of weight loss* directly and controllably improve health?

Not necessarily. Healthy eating, healthy exercise and healthy living are not just about weight. Instead, "healthy" is completely, 100% up to you (and me) to define and goes far beyond that number on the scale.

In my recovery, as I began to focus less on the number, "healthy" began to mean things like:

- Being able to go to Whole Foods and eat something off the hot bar—even though I hated the thought of eating canola oil.

- Going with the flow to whatever restaurant my friends chose—and finding something to nosh on.

- Not having to call ahead to the hotel before I got there on vacation to find out where the closest gym was.

- Not packing my week's worth of meals in my suitcase for that same vacation (again, going with the flow).

- Letting my mom cook dinner for my family—instead of me having to do it, or having a completely separate meal.

- Experimenting with making a homemade almond butter cookie (it may not be a regular sugar cookie, but it was a cookie—a treat).

- Taking a bite of a thoughtfully-made cookie from a friend (even though I feared sugar).

- Not having to buy everything organic.

- Being okay with less than an hour in the gym some days.

- Being okay with an early morning meeting or 6 am flight that left me without my usual morning gym time.

- Laughing…smiling…playing…being at peace.

Although weighing a "healthy" weight was *also* part of my recovery from disordered eating, ironically, the *less* I began focusing on the number on the scale, and *more* on self-care and self-love, the more freedom, liberty and peace (with myself) I found.

Kind of like the saying: "Love finds you when you least expect it," when you stop trying so hard to be a perfect weight or attain a weight range or body type that you approve of, the more peace, contentment and happiness (in your own skin) finds you.

Restoration

Sleep and rest, or "restoration" are vital for intuition and connection to your body. In fact, your brain capacity is equivalent to being legally intoxicated when you sleep less than six hours. Your reaction time, thought processing, motivation and awareness all slow down.

Like a plant needs water or a car needs gas, you and I flourish when our basic needs of food, water, movement, low stress and rest are met. As crazy simple as it sounds, these factors won't steer you wrong when it comes to thriving and reigniting intuition.

Sleep
One-third of Americans get less than six hours of sleep.

Less than six hours of sleep **reduces our natural mortality by approximately 25%**—a higher percentage than any of the following risk factors:

- Obesity (reduces mortality by 18%)
- Sedentary lifestyle (reduces mortality by 16%)
- Not eating all your veggies (reduces mortality by 5%).

Statistics aside, **lack of sleep is directly linked to:**

- Constipation and lack of full-elimination
- Bloating
- Suppressed appetite or Insatiable appetite
- Poor workouts and recovery
- Inability to build muscle or tone
- Stomach cramps and pains
- Lowered mood
- Brain fog
- Headaches

Are you getting enough sleep? General **sleep recommendations** from the Sleep Foundation, include:

- Newborns (0-3 months): 14-17 hours
- Infants (4-11 months): 12-15 hours
- Toddlers (1-2 years): 11-14 hours
- Preschoolers (3-5): 10-13 hours
- School age children (6-13): 9-11 hours
- Teenagers (14-17): 8-10 hours
- Younger adults (18-25): 7-9 hours
- Adults (26-64): 7-9 hours
- Older adults (65+): 7-8 hours

Sleep does a body good, and not just any sleep, but QUALITY sleep.

In my eating disorder and even "youthful college years, I simply "didn't have time" for sleep. If I wanted to workout 7 - 8 hours per day, participate in every club under the sun, and soak up the moments, sleep came second—until I hit a wall.

My body broke down, and as if I got hit by a truck, it no longer could keep up with that same old pace (and actually function).

If there's one thing I've learned since I started making sleep a necessity in life, it's that I am not invincible! I require sleep to be **more productive, functional, vibrant, healthy and energetic throughout my days.**

How to get into a new sleep routine if under-sleeping has become your norm?

Here are some simple ways to improve your sleep hygiene:

- **De-brighten.** Sure, we hear about how "bad" screens are for us—iPhones, laptops, TVs—especially at night, but we still use them. (An estimated 95% of Americans regularly use screens shortly before going to sleep). Bright artificial light messes with our circadian rhythm cycle and can throw off your sleep-wake cycle, as well as stress your hormones and adrenals out. If you are adamant about keeping up your screen time in the evenings, consider de-brightening the blue-light on your screens. Check out the "**Just get flux**" app—designed to shift your screen to a more natural light, depending on the time of day. Or grab a pair of orange-tinted indoor sunglasses for their blue-light blocking effects. Amazon sells various versions, designed to give your eyes and body a break from the harsh lighting from screens.

  Q. Why is blue light "so bad?" The light from our screens is "short-wavelength-enriched," meaning it has a higher concentration of blue light than natural light, and this blue light affects our levels of melatonin (a sleep-inducing hormone) more than any other wavelength. When this happens, changes in sleep patterns mess with our natural circadian rhythms— throwing our bodies and our metabolic processes completely off.

- **Candle Down.** Dim down the lights at night, and establish a "candling down" ritual, such as unplugging from electronics in favor of reading, writing, reflecting, praying, meditating, listening to music, and gratitude. This practice can help you (and your body) get ready for bed both physically and mentally.

- **Warm Up.** Coming out of a warm shower and into a cooler bedroom will cause a slight decrease in body temperature, a drop that scientifically helps trigger a tranquil, drowsy feeling by slowing down essential metabolic activities.

- **Cool the Room Off.** The body goes hard to work while you slumber—sleep is when recovery, repair and restoration processes happen (meaning your metabolism fires up!). Your body temp naturally rises at night, making a cool home and sleep environment crucial to quality sleep. Also, a cooler environment induces a drop in your own core temperature, triggering your body's "let's hit the sack" (and sleep through the night) button. The ideal temp? Somewhere around 60-68 degrees.

- **Black it Out.** Just like blue light is not conducive to winding down at night, light while we actually sleep isn't good, either—even light seeping in through the windows from the street lights, your phone or alarm clock. Why? Similar to blue light. Light in general at night throws our circadian rhythms off. Keep your body in a deep-sleep mode with some blackout curtains.

- **Think Happy Thoughts.** Prep your body for sweet dreams with one of these rituals: 1) Listen to soothing, relaxing and pleasant sounds or music bed; 2) Spritz your body or lather on some good smelling essential oils (like peppermint and lavender); 3) Think happy thoughts before bed. Instead of worrying about your bank account or some work to-do that won't be resolved tonight, choose to fix your eyes on something you're grateful for or something positive and happy.

- **Rise with the Sun.** Back in the day, the sun was the natural alarm clock for most folks. Since we no longer sleep outside (and thanks to Edison and the lightbulb), lights often go on before the sun does. Aim to stick as close to your body's natural circadian rhythms by "rising with the sun." I love my "Natural Sun" **Phillips Wake-Up Light Alarm**—programmed to mimic the sun rising in my room (no matter what time I need to get up). I can't imagine going back to a regular buzzing alarm clock and feeling like a firefighter going on a call in the middle of the night with my old alarm clock. Also, check out the **Sleep Cycle** app, which analyzes your sleep throughout the night, and when it's time to wake up, the app wakes you up in your lightest sleep phase for easier and more refreshed waking.

- **A Little Bit More.** Does getting more sleep still seem hard to do? If you are 'under-sleeping' right now, start small: Aim for just 20-30 minutes more, or 1-2 hours more on the weekends. In addition, power naps between 5-20 minutes can serve as a re-charge to your body (More than that may make you feel groggy). And, lastly, little by little, readjust your thinking to: *I don't have time NOT to sleep*.

Rest

Rest is one of the most often overlooked components in self-care and intuition. Unlike sleep, rest—making time for play, restoration and rejuvenation—seems far more like a luxury, rather than a necessity. I used to hate the idea of rest. In my mind, I thought rest meant: "Lazy," "Bored," or "Unproductive." However, like sleep, we also *"recharge"* when we have time away from work, stress, demands or pressure. Rest allows us to tune out distractions and reconnect with our intuition

How do you rest? Do you make time for rest?

One of my favorite examples of the power of rest is Thomas Edison. Thomas Edison is known as one of the greatest inventors who ever lived. He invented the phonograph, the motion picture and, of course, the light bulb. In total, Edison had 1,093 patents to his name. As brilliant of an innovator as Edison was though, he was also the worst fisherman. Edison used to spend an hour almost everyday, alone, sitting at the end of a dock and fish, but, he never caught any fish.

*People often wondered: "**Why is Edison so obsessed with fishing when he is so bad at it?**" Later in life, a friend actually asked Edison the reason behind him being such a lousy fisherman.*

"I really never caught any fish because I have never used any bait," Edison said.

"Why in the world would you fish without bait?" his friend asked back.

*To which Edison replied, "Because when you fish without bait, people don't bother you and neither do the fish. **It provides me my best time to think**."*

We all have a need for rest, or recovery—not only from physical exertion, but mental and emotional exertion as well, and, when we get it, we can be more in touch with ourselves. "Rest" does not always equate to "sitting on a couch" or sleeping either. Rest is achieved in a variety of ways.

For instance, if you've been sitting at your desk most of the day, "rest" may look like disconnecting from the screen for some time spent outside in the sun, or hitting up a spin class. Training hard for a big race or pushing it in the gym? Rest may mean taking an "active rest" or recovery day for a yoga class or to meet a friend for a walk. Tend to burn a candle at both ends or keep a busy social calendar? "Rest" may look like having a night to yourself to re-charge, or for those who have not been social at all, "rest" could be "re-energizing" by spending time with others. Ever been stuck in a food or fitness rut—keeping yourself bound to a diet, a routine, overtraining? Rest may look like giving yourself permission to stop the madness and do or something different.

Rest is often a contrast—the opposite—of what you've been doing.

Such as going from a period of intense creativity to a mental task that is more linear, like checking email or cleaning your house. If you've been analyzing and over-thinking, break it up with painting, doodling, creating and imagining. Instead of listening, try talking. If you've been doing, try thinking. Like sleep, rest is essential to reawakening your own gut intuition for self-care.

Reflections & Rule Break Project:

1. **Take a "rest" inventory:** Consider the ways you incorporate rest right now (and the ways you do not). What does rest look like or mean for you?

2. **Make a list of rejuvenating or restful activities and practices** you like to do. Stumped? Think about what you liked to do as a kid, or what activities you do and find yourself feeling a release from stress, worry or work.

3. **Make rest or "you time" a priority**—just like you do your work, workouts, or even the "unhealthy" routines you kept up before. How can you work "rest" into your calendar> Schedule time for rest, or "you" time, just as you schedule time for other necessities. Most every day in my calendar, I set aside some time to do there things: 10 to 20 minutes of time in my morning devotional and prayer, one hour for writing and creativity, and one hour for my daily movement or workout. These are practically non-negotiable for me to recharge. If it seems like other conflicts or events try to take over, put your

foot down and don't let them. And, if this seems daunting, start with baby steps—perhaps just 5-10 minutes a day, or a day of rest on a Saturday or Sunday to recharge.

4. **Set a Reminder.** Every day at noon, a reminder goes off on my phone that simply says, "Pray." A sticky note on my dashboard of my car reads, "Be still and know that I am God." I have another reminder at 8 p.m. that says, "Unplug." Keep reminders for yourself!

5. **Have fun with it.** How can you begin to shift your mentality from "rest is for lazy people" or "rest is boring" to "rest is energizing and fun"? Remember: Rest is so much more than just watching reruns of *Gilmore Girls* (although it totally can be!).

Stress Busting

Speaking of rest and rejuvenation, it's time we have a heart-to-heart about stress.

Stress is the number one culprit of all disease and a leading culprit against your ability to be in touch with your body and yourself. According to the American Psychological Foundation, **75% of Americans report regularly experiencing stress**—with nearly 50% of people saying stress keeps them awake at night.

When you typically think of stress, you may think of mental and emotional stress. However, stress is actually defined as "any event in which environmental demands, internal demands, or both tax or exceed the adaptive resources of an individual." Any event that causes increased demands or "allostatic load" to your body's stress— it does not have to be psychological or emotional.

You can be totally carefree on a beach somewhere and have "everything going for you," in the world, but still be "under stress" if you have a zinc deficiency, leaky gut acne and undiagnosed food intolerances.

There are 4 primary triggers that set off your stress response:

1. **Perceived Stress.**
   Relationship difficulties, financial strain, work demands, walking down a dark alley at night, public speaking, flying in airplanes, fear of heights, isolation, dieting mentality. Inner mean girl chronic illness (feeling out of control), or any event perceived as *harmful and uncontrollable.*

2. **Circadian Rhythm Disruption.**
   High coffee and caffeine consumption. Blue light (LED Light) exposure—particularly at night. Sleeping with phone lights and night lights in our rooms. Lack of sleep. Shift work. Phone/screen time usage at all hours. Working out late at night or super early without enough rest.

3. **Inflammation.**
   Any source of inflammation is a chronic stressor. Gut-microbiome disruption or leaky gut. Nutrient deficiencies. Side effects of prednisone and other steroid drugs. Antibiotic, NSAIDs and long-term medication use. Chronic elevations of cortisol. Toxic hygiene and cleaning products. Smoking. Overtraining (inflames hormones). Sedentary lifestyles. Gut pathogens like E. coli. Food intolerances. Environmental toxins. Pesticides and GMOs. Impaired thyroid function.

4. **Blood Sugar Dysregulation.**
   Often due to nutrient imbalances. Symptoms include: Low blood sugar. Sugar cravings. Low fat diets. Low protein diets. Impaired glucose sensing in the hypothalamus (type 2 diabetes and metabolic syndrome). Headaches. Craving comfort foods when you're stressed out.

If any one or multiple triggers of stress are present (and remain present for an extended period), or your body is overloaded with multiple stressors with little recovery, a "chronic stress response" occurs and your ability to adapt to that stress (and connect to your body)goes way down.

Stress manifests itself in a variety of ways. Some people experience high blood pressure, chest pain or digestive dysfunction. Others get anxiety, constant worry, or knots in their stomach. And, still, others have inflammation, skin breakouts, heart palpitations, headaches, back-aches, insomnia, decreased metabolism, autoimmune conditions, SIBO and other gut pathologies—you name a chronic disease, inflammatory response or physical or mental discomfort, and you'll most likely find stress as the culprit behind it.

What to Do About Stress

Stress is unavoidable, yet it IS manageable. Your response to stress greatly impacts your outcomes and can help you begin attuning to your bod. Some examples of stress-**management** include:

Behavior & Lifestyle Modification
You can't supplement your way out of stress, *especially* if there is a strong behavioral or lifestyle component. Behavior and lifestyle mod-ifications are vast and entail everything from a healthy diet, to a mod-erately active lifestyle, intuitive eating, eliminating toxins (in your envi-ronment and food sources), chewing your food and slowing down at meals, to incorporating more work-life balance, learning your own boundaries, making time for play and connection with other people, doing things you love and starting your day off with a positive morn-ing routine. Therapeutic support and mindfulness-based stress reduc-tion techniques (meditation, yoga, tai chi) may also prove beneficial for the emotional and behavioral stress management.

Circadian Reset
Eliminating blue-light use at night is a no-brainer here. Thankfully, today, there is an app for that! Additionally, amber-tinted glasses help reduce blue light in the evening hours, along with keeping elec-tronic devices away from you while you sleep, darkening your room

completely, and requesting constant shifts (as opposed to alternating schedules) if you work some overnights or some days. As for coffee, limiting it to 1 cup of quality coffee per day (a fresh, dark organic roast) is highly recommended (caffeine has a major impact on the HPA axis and sleep, and most Americans drink 2-3 cups per day).

Inflammation & Blood Sugar "Re-regulation"

These two go hand and hand and are most often addressed through an individualized treatment protocol of the stress—such as healing underlying gut pathologies like bacterial overgrowth or a thyroid condition. Also, dietary changes also play a significant role here, such as increasing fatty acid intake through food and a cod liver oil supplement, or replacing a grain-based diet with a more balanced diet inclusive to proteins, fats and a mix of fibrous and starchy vegetables.

Reflection & Exercise:

Assess the current stressors in your life—anything from the 9 to 5 job you hate, the workout routine you keep, the 2-3 cups of coffee you drink, or the 6 hours of sleep you typically get each night. Make a list. Then brainstorm specific de-stressors you can incorporate to diminish stress. Pick one or two action items to start with.

Remember: not all stress is bad—it's a part of life. It only becomes "bad" when it persists without relief or balance.

Here are some of the de-stressors I came up with for myself. Try some of mine or create your own list.

Reducing Exposure to Stress:

- Limit the to-do list
- Just say "no"
- Turn off the news
- Unplug
- Fill my life with positive people, not toxic relationships
- Manage my time wisely

- Reduce light exposure at night
- Cut back/cut out coffee
- Get plenty of sleep
- Replace plastic tupperware and water bottles with glassware and stainless steel, and use additive and toxin-free cleaning and hygiene products

Minimizing Stress I Can't Avoid:

- Practice the power of positive thinking
- Delegate tasks (ex. instead of spending 20 hours working on a website issue, hire someone to do the 2-3 hours of work)
- Do one thing at a time
- Use positive self-affirmations
- Lower my expectations and standards—perfection does not exist
- Reframe all situations and get in someone else's shoes
- Pray or meditate instead of worrying

New Tools & Strategies:

- Do things I love more often
- Pick up or try out a new hobby
- Baby steps—try just incorporating one stress-management technique at a time
- Pencil it in—make a date with yourself and celebrate you
- Try meditation or yoga
- Get back into nature
- Use essential oils diffused around the home
- Play—whatever that means to you
- Exercise or join a group fitness class (30-60/minutes most days of movement)

Pick one to two things to get started and go with it. Small simple actions pave the way to big intuitive results—in all areas.

Step 3

Redefine

Intuition in Practice

I hate directions. Give me a manual for assembling a table or directions to completing an assignment and I tend to skim over them more than reading.

I learn by **doing**. Getting my hands dirty and "just doing it."

My recovery process (freedom from my obsessive food struggles, over-exercise, body-image get-ups and NOT listening to my body) was the same way.

I only learned by *doing*.

After spending a year in eating disorder treatment being told what to eat, when to move, and how to think differently, ***real recovery began.*** As I was released back to the "real world," I had one of two options:

1. Run back to my eating disorder—the world that was comfortable and the way of living I knew like the back of my hand; or
2. Jump in head first and do something different (i.e. trusting my body).

I *wanted* something different.

Enter: Redefine

With all this NEW information, I needed to completely redefine what my new, intuitive life and health *actually looked like* on a day-to-day and meal-to-meal basis.

From what I ate to how I talked to myself, my daily workouts, my career path, and how I spent my energy and time. Things in my "new life" had to look different if I wanted to change.

Things like:

- No longer listening to my "Inner Mean Girl"
- Making peace with food and nourishing my body with balanced eating
- Working out to build my body up—not break it down
- Canceling my fitness and body-focused magazine subscriptions
- Connecting to my faith and God and surrendering my struggles up to Him
- Finding real friends and surrounding myself with a supportive community
- Living by a new motto to "do what I love and love what I do"—despite any fears
- Pursuing the passions and purpose I'd discovered in my soul-searching
- Ultimately, no longer living out the definition of "insanity"— doing the same things over and over and expecting a different result.

Doing things differently and choosing to start trusting my body.

Now that you've gained a bigger vision of food, body and fitness freedom, and raised awareness to old lies and new truths in ALL areas of your life, it is time to bring these insights together to "redefine" the **HOW**.

HOW to live out "being more intuitive" after all this change talk and information in our Gain Vision and Raise Awareness Steps?!

HOW do you eat, **HOW** do you workout, and **HOW** do you REALLY see yourself and think differently, intuitively?

Most diets, fitness trainers or recovery programs may call this section "the aCTION plan," "the diet," "the treatment," or "the program," but I don't believe in just telling you exactly what to eat, what diet to follow, what ab exercises to do, or what affirmations to say.

Instead,. ALL you have to focus on is ONE thing.

I call it **The Check-In**—checking in with the core of your heart, mind and gut.

The Check In

Plans and diet rules are gone! **The Check-In Method** will help you never need to count another calorie, overthinking what you should have for dinner, or earn your pizza on the treadmill again.

How to do it?

Ask yourself these three questions:

1. **How do I *feel*?**
2. **What is my *truth*?**
3. **What would *thriving me* do?**

That's it.

To help you get started, you are encouraged to keep a **Mindful Eating, Movement & Mindset** log in your daily journal for at least for 3 to 14 days. While this is not necessary, this activity can be tremendously insightful and help rewire intuitive thinking, eating, moving, and being to become more automatic.

Around meals, your mindful log will include:

- What you ate and drank
- The time you ate
- Level of hunger on a scale 1-10 before you begin the mean and your level of fullness after on the same scale.
- How you felt before and after eating (physically, mentally, emotionally)
- Any additional notes you have about thoughts, feelings, or food

Here's an example of the **Hunger-Fullness scale** you'll be using to assess your hunger and fullness before meals, as well as a daily template of your food log:

On a scale of 1-10, rate your level of hunger before a meal (1=famished, 10=stuffed), then rate your level of fullness after eating. Make sure to note any physical feelings, emotions or thoughts you have around meals. No calorie counting or macros needed.

Date:

Breakfast:
Hunger (Before)
Fullness (After)
Mood, Physical, Mental Notes:
Time:

Lunch:
Hunger (Before)
Fullness (After)
Mood, Physical, Mental Notes:
Time:

Dinner:
Hunger (Before)
Fullness (After)
Mood, Physical, Mental Notes:
Time:

Snacks:
Times:

Total Water Intake:

Exercise/Movement (if any):

Sleep (Night Before; Hours & Time)

Additional Notes:

Here are a couple more things to think about which you can add to your journal.

- Clear the clutter in your mind—prioritize the top 3 things (only 3) you'd like to accomplish in a given day to keep focused and aligned with your personal mission and passions.
- Reflect and record the top 3 things you learned or cool things that happened on a given day to practice gratitude and a positive mindset.

You are encouraged to connect with your body and mind in other ways, too. You don't need more rules, macro or calories to hit, or a workout plan to do.

All you need is these three questions and to "let go" to let the body lead the way:

1. **Does this align with who am I? (heart)**
2. **What is my truth? (mind)**

3. **How do I feel? (gut)**

Focus on one thing at a time and start right now.

Shhh...Your body is speaking. Are you listening?

Breaking & Making Your Own Rules: To 80/20 Balance & Beyond!

One challenge for you as we go our separate ways.

Today, do one thing.

One thing that may be completely different than you've been doing in relation to food, your body, fitness, or your routine lifestyle.

In other words, break one rule. Any rule you choose.

- Let go of your time constraints around meal times. Ask your body when it wants to eat instead.

- Just say "no" to overcommitments, overtraining or under-eating.

- Delete your calorie tracking app.

- Eat a sweet potato with dinner (after your "no carbs after noon" cut off)

- Try a bite of something new.

- Allow yourself to eat even if you don't workout "super hard," or if you don't workout at all.

- Bust a food rut. Cook something new. Try a new veggie.

- Use real ghee or butter instead of cooking spray.

- Add protein to your meal if you usually skimp, or try a veggie-based meal if your body just feels like a veggie soup.

- Say "yes" to lunchtime with a friend if you typically avoid eating with others, or "yes" to cooking in if you never do.

- Or (my personal favorite), whip up your own rendition of Mickey Mouse pancakes (with bananas and dark chocolate chips, of course).

Want support in redefining what intuition looks like in action for you?

Visit DrLauryn.com to connect with Dr. Lauryn Lax's Virtual Thrive Clinic and check out her books and online programs, with tons of tools, resources and strategies for transforming your health and mindset, and helping you along your own journey of intuitive living, eating, moving and believing in yourself.

Author Bio:
Dr. Lauryn Lax, OTR/L, NTP

Who Am I?

- Doctor of Occupational Therapy (Belmont University)
- Nutritional Therapy Practitioner (Nutritional Therapy Association)
- Institute for Functional Medicine (AFMCP)
- B.A. Journalism/Communications (University of Texas)
- Certified Fitness Professional (ACE, CrossFit Level I)

What Do I Do?

- Functional Medicine
- Nutritional Therapy
- Counseling, Coaching & Occupational Therapy
- Eating Disorder Recovery Coaching

The Real Me:

- I love mornings
- Mondays are my favorite day of the week
- Julia Roberts (actress) and I share the same birthday
- As a kid, I wanted to be a writer and the "next" Katie Couric on the Today Show
- My biggest pet peeves are wasting time and traffic
- Country and boy-band music from the 90's gets me singing and dancing
- I grew up in Arkansas
- Austin, Texas is my favorite place on earth
- I pick the beach over mountains any day!
- I love volunteering with kids and visiting older people in the nursing home
- I have an Amazon Prime addiction (I love reading new books!)

Resources:

As for tools and online resources, I primarily use these tests for assessing Character Strengths:

- Strengths Finder (Gallup Strengths) https://www.gallup-strengthscenter.com/Purchase/en-US/Product
- The VIA Character Survey https://www.viacharacter.org
- Myers Briggs http://www.myersbriggs.org
- Enneagram https://www.enneagraminstitute.com

Warren, Rick. (2015). SHAPE Assessment. http://www.where-newlifebegins.org/hp_wordpress/wp-content/uploads/2015/08/SHAPE-Assessment.pdf

http://www.gallup.com/poll/107692/social-time-crucial-daily-emotional-wellbeing.aspx

Andrade, C., & Radhakrishnan, R. (2009): research review of nearly 50 research studies on the impacts of faith on healing

Thrive's Pick Six was inspired by Dale Carnegie's classic How to Win Friends & Influence People.

Bradberry, T. (2016). How Being Busy Makes You Unproductive. Forbes.

Campos JJ, Kermoian R, Zumbahlen MR. Socioemotional transformations in the family system following infant crawling onset. In: Eisenberg N, Fabes RA, editors. Emotion and its regulation in early development. San Francisco: Jossey-Bass; 1992. Pp. 25–40.

Carnegie, D. (1936). How to Win Friends and Influence People. Pocket Books.

Chopra, K. (2012). Impact of positive self-talk. University of Lethbridge. Faculty of Education. https://www.uleth.ca/dspace/handle/10133/3202

Hatzigeorgiadis, A. Zourbanos, N., Galanis, E., Theodorakis, Y. (2011). Self-Talk and Sports Performance. Perspectives on Psychological Science . 6 (4): 348 - 356. doi: 10.1177/1745691611413136.

Keizer A1, Smeets MA, Dijkerman HC, Uzunbajakau SA, van Elburg A, Postma A. (2013). Too fat to fit through the door: first evidence for disturbed body-scaled action in anorexia nervosa during locomotion. PLoS One. 8(5). doi: 10.1371/journal.pone.0064602

Lagattuta KH, Wellman HM. Differences in early parent-child conversations about negative versus positive emotions: Implications for the development of psychological understanding. Developmental Psychology. 2002;38:564–580.

Leuchter AF1, Cook IA, Witte EA, Morgan M, Abrams M. (2002). Changes in brain function of depressed subjects during treatment with placebo. American Journal of Psychology. Am J Psychiatry. 2002 Jan;

Rubinstein, J. S., Meyer, D. E. & Evans, J. E. (2001). Executive Control of Cognitive Processes in Task Switching. Journal of Experimental Psychology: Human Perception and Performance, 27, 763-797.

Vaish, A., Grossmann, T., & Woodward, A. (2008). Not all emotions are created equal: The negativity bias in social-emotional development. Psychological Bulletin, 134(3), 383–403. http://doi.org/10.1037/0033-2909.134.3.383

http://atrantil.com
http://www.sleepcycle.com
Cappuccio, F. P., D'Elia, L., Strazzullo, P., & Miller, M. A. (2010). Sleep Duration and All-Cause Mortality: A Systematic Review and Meta-Analysis of Prospective Studies. Sleep, 33(5), 585–592.

Centers for Disease Control. CDC. (2016). 1 in 3 adults doesn't get enough sleep. CDC Newsroom. https://www.cdc.gov/media/releases/2016/p0215-enough-sleep.html.

Ganasegeran, K., Al-Dubai, S.AR., Quereshi, A., AA Al-abed, AM, R., Aljunid, SJ. (2012). Social and psychological factors affecting eating habits among university students in a Malaysian medical school: a cross-sectional study. Nutrition Journal. https://doi.org/10.1186/1475-2891-11-48

Higgs, S. & Thomas, J. (2016). Social influences on eating. Current Opinion in Human Behavioral Sciences; 9: 1-6. https://doi.org/10.1016/j.cobeha.2015.10.005

Ingraham, P. (2017). Strength Training Frequency. Pain Science. https://www.painscience.com/articles/strength-training-frequency.php

Li K, Kaaks R, Linseisen J, et al. (2012). Associations of dietary calcium intake and calcium supplementation with myocardial infarction and stroke risk and overall cardiovascular mortality in the Heidelberg cohort of the European Prospective Investigation into Cancer and Nutrition study (EPIC-Heidelberg). Heart; 98:920-925.

Wang, Q.; Afshin, A.; Yakoob, MY; Singh, GM.; Rehm, CD.; Khatibzadeh, S.; Micha, R.; Shi, P. & Mozaffarian, D. The Global Burden of Diseases Nutrition and Chronic Diseases Expert Group (NutriCoDE). (2016). Impact of Nonoptimal Intakes of Saturated, Polyunsaturated, and Trans Fat on Global Burdens of Coronary Heart Disease. Journal of the American Heart Association. https://doi.org/10.1161/JAHA.115.002891

Li K, Kaaks R, Linseisen J, et al, 2012

Weatherby, D. (2004). Signs and Symptoms Analysis from a Functional Perspective. Emperors Group LLC.

Williamson, A., & Feyer, A. (2000). Moderate sleep deprivation produces impairments in cognitive and motor performance equivalent to legally prescribed levels of alcohol intoxication. Occupational and Environmental Medicine. 57 (10). http://dx.doi.org/10.1136/oem.57.10.649

Bohon, C., & Stice, E. (2012). Negative Affect and Neural Response to Palatable Food Intake in Bulimia Nervosa. Appetite, 58(3), 964–970. http://doi.org/10.1016/j.appet.2012.02.051

Van Oudenhove, L., McKie, S., Lassman, D., Uddin, B., Paine, P., Coen, S., … Aziz, Q. (2011). Fatty acid–induced gut-brain signaling attenuates neural and behavioral effects of sad emotion in humans. The Journal of Clinical Investigation, 121(8), 3094–3099. http://doi.org/10.1172/JCI46380